Paranoid Finance

Theory Redux series
Series editor: Laurent de Sutter

Published Titles

Paranoid Finance

Fabian Muniesa

polity

The right of Fabian Muniesa to be identified as Author of this Work has been asserted in accordance with the UK Copyright, Designs and Patents Act 1988.

First published in 2024 by Polity Press

Polity Press
65 Bridge Street
Cambridge CB2 1UR, UK

Polity Press
111 River Street
Hoboken, NJ 07030, USA

ISBN-13: 978-1-5095-6116-2
ISBN-13: 978-1-5095-6117-9 (pb)

A catalogue record for this book is available from the British Library.

Library of Congress Control Number: 2024934243

Typeset in 12.5 on 15pt Adobe Garamond
by Cheshire Typesetting Ltd, Cuddington, Cheshire
Printed and bound in Great Britain by CPI Group (UK) Ltd, Croydon

The publisher has used its best endeavors to ensure that the URLs for external websites referred to in this book are correct and active at the time of going to press. However, the publisher has no responsibility for the websites and can make no guarantee that a site will remain live or that the content is or will remain appropriate.

Every effort has been made to trace all copyright holders, but if any have been overlooked the publisher will be pleased to include any necessary credits in any subsequent reprint or edition.

For further information on Polity, visit our website:
politybooks.com

Contents

Acknowledgments

Numerous colleagues ought to be thanked for sharing helpful comments, ideas and references, and for offering opportunities for discussion. These include: Marie Alauzen, Jens Beckert, Elena Bogdanova, Théo Bourgeron, Yves Citton, Béatrice Cointe, Barbara Czarniawska, Jean Daniélou, Liliana Doganova, Marion Fourcade, Oz Frankel, Daniel Fridman, Clément Gasull, Susi Geiger, Jonathan Harris, Geraldine Juárez, Hyo Yoon Kang, Peter Knight, Aris Komporozos-Athanasiou, Martijn Konings, Javier Lezaun, Dominique Linhardt, Andreas Mayer, Nadia Matringe, Liz McFall, Afshin Mehrpouya, Andrea Mennicken, Gemma Milne, James Christopher Mizes, Leigh Mueller, Horacio Ortiz, José

Ossandón, Anna Paretskaya, Michael Power, Emily Rosamond, Amin Samman, Michele Spanò, Laurent de Sutter, John Thompson, Giacomo Todeschini, Alexandre Violle, Désirée Waibel and Leon Wansleben.

This book expands on an article titled "Paranoid finance" published earlier in *Social Research: An International Quarterly* (vol. 89, no. 3, Fall 2022, pages 731–56), as part of a special issue titled *Conspiracy Thinking*, edited by Oz Frankel. Permissions have kindly been granted by the editor and the publisher, Johns Hopkins University Press.

Introduction

Finance is a semiotic engine. It produces meaning, and that meaning is troubling. For sure, properly considered, finance is rather about producing money. It is about producing money with money, and about the power to do so. But this works as long as that money and that power are signified appropriately. Finance is indeed a legitimation game, an ideology. It is a process of justification and critique, a process of reference. Finance is a way of thinking and of making sense of things, a worldview full of narratives about what is right and what is wrong, and about what to do accordingly.

So what is it that is troubling about that? At the heart of this engine lies indeed a dangerous idea. A vernacular notion that controls the moral appraisal and political determination of things. This is the idea of value. Of value and "value creation." This seems innocuous and rather clever at first sight. Value that ought to be created through the virtuous and intelligent management of money. Value that should be assessed from the perspective of a skillful, emancipated investor who understands capital and cares for its yield. Value that must derive from the future, and the anticipation of which requires responsibility, precaution and foresight. A notion inherited from the traditions of liberal philosophy and political economy, which carries the marks of normative disquisitions about the foundations of true value and the perils of false value. So value is good, and value creation even more so.

When taken lightly, this idea of value creation works quite openly as a kind of a euphemism for the mundane idea of making money. It is good for the corporate brochure, for the finance lecture or for the political rally. But then the elementary problems of the who, the why, the how and the for what of that moneymaking can do without it. It is when taken too seriously that the trouble of its signification emerges. Considering things exclusively and forcefully in the terms of value precipitates an array of unsettling concerns that can only be fully dealt with within a delusional space. Where does value come from, ultimately? From which kind of supreme force? From us? From me? Is this value true? Is it invisible? Is it magical? Am I entitled to it? How shall I protect it? What threatens it? Who is taking it away from me? Extremist, fundamentalist interpretations of value creation produce monsters. And these are the monsters of finance.

Of course, the terminologies of value are manifold and they extend well beyond the area examined here, which is the area of value understood as an economic thing. Value is certainly a messy notion. It can refer, for instance, to the denomination of the outcome of measurement, as when one talks of the value of a variable. It can also mean a standard of conduct or a moral principle, as when people are said to have values – or told that they ought to have them – and act accordingly, or not. It can, in addition, denote significance and importance, implying that something of value is worthy of consideration, held dear or signaled as superior. And all these meanings do often mingle with each other, and with others. The purpose here is not to intervene in this terminological mess with a clarification. On the contrary, the definitional quandaries of value form here a vernacular problem: a piece of empirical reality, a concept immanent in a particular worldview, surely not an analytical category.

There is one particular kernel within this mess – just one among others, but a most consequential one: one that leads directly to wealth, fortune and treasure, and, therefore, to the crafts of moneymaking. This is finance, broadly conceived. There is an element of technical measure there: financial valuation, that is, in the sense, for instance, of gauging the profitability of an investment opportunity. And there is a moral pattern too: the imperative of the optimization, intensification and fructification of money, and the idea that creating value, as this process is called, is a good thing for society. And there is also a sense of recognition, weight and fundament: what things are worth depends on their capacity to generate or represent that value, and what persons are worth depends on their faculty to claim or obtain that value. What that value is exactly (what it consists of, where it comes from, where it goes) is surely not settled. But it becomes recognizable, somehow, when put against the background of what threatens it.

In order to just make sense, the notion of value requires in fact a perimeter of non-value: a space of waste, liability and dilapidation, a territory where the enemies of value operate, propagating false, spurious value. A fence needs then to be established in order to secure veritable value creation and protect its foundations. But those foundations are nowhere to be found. Value acquires the features of a spiraling reference, a vanishing substance, a phantasm. The promise of future return becomes an obsession. The ideal of the free investor prompts a damaging subjectivity. The spiritual element of capital turns into a nightmare.

The hypothesis developed here is that the categories of financial imagination contain, indeed, a paranoid kernel. This question can certainly be examined from a variety of angles, and the pages that follow are focused on a specific one. This is about looking at radical views of financial value within contemporary conspiratorial, millennialist thinking, and signaling there the consequences of mainstream financial imagination.

To be sure, talking today about conspiracy fantasies often means talking about the restoration of truth. About telling the rational from the irrational, and the mad from the sane. The approach adopted here is different. Fantasy features in these pages as an element of reality whose meaning – whose rationality – requires attention. It features as a symptom that reveals something troubling already at work within the perimeter of ordinary financial culture. Paranoid finance – short for the radicalized, fantasized, disturbed expression of financial ideals of value – is not considered here as a delusional deformation of a standard financial rationality that would be sound in nature, but, rather, as a cultural syndrome that makes the paranoid potential of mainstream financial discourse explicit.

The essay is short. It draws from studies and ideas offered previously elsewhere (Muniesa 2014, 2016, 2017a, 2017b, 2020, 2022, 2023a, 2023b, 2023c). The purpose here is not to delve into academic disquisitions about disciplinary boundaries, methodological precautions and empirical contexts. The purpose is to go to the point: to refine an argument, to defend its radicalness, and to clarify its consequences – its consequences, most especially, for the critique of finance. It is also, in part, about expanding and making more explicit an earlier, incipient – and perhaps too condensed – formulation of the idea of "paranoid finance" (Muniesa 2022).

The next chapter ("The trouble with financial imagination") unpacks what it means to claim that finance is a semiotic engine, and that the meaning of financial value is inherently troubling. The chapter after that ("A radicalization of value") documents the financial element in contemporary conspiratorial cultures, with particular attention to the QAnon syndrome and to comparable strains of extremist fantasies of sovereign value. Next is a chapter ("Tensions within the mainstream") in which the connections between paranoid finance and standard financial imagination are spelled out, demonstrating the inherent trouble contained in financial value. The last chapter ("The critique of finance") observes how critical discourse often remains within the perimeter of financial imagination, opening the way to paranoid finance, and asks how that spell can be broken.

The trouble with financial imagination

In their *Capitalism and Schizophrenia*, Gilles Deleuze and Félix Guattari (1983, 1987) put together a series of challenging intuitions that are of relevance here. The reader may feel that the promise of a link between capitalism and schizophrenia proper is, as such, often lost in their pages to the benefit of other seemingly unrelated disquisitions. But the link is there. Their investigation is distinctively about what they call regimes of signs. Signs are apparatuses. Signification is an operation. And this operation amounts to some kind of an orchestration, a process of institutional sedimentation that can be characterized in the terms of a specific political disposition. A regime of signs can, hence, be more or less authoritarian, or more or less libertarian, depending on how the semiotic connection to a reference – eventually ultimate and foundational, or, conversely, evasive and groundless – is arranged within this regime. And this is also about the production of subjectivity. A regime of signs may be, then, more or less psychotic, or more or less neurotic, prompting distinctive paths – sometimes spiraling, sometimes fractured – for interpretation.

And capitalism is a regime of signs. Capital features there in that guise, quite explicitly considered as a semiotic engine. Turning things into capital is indeed a signification process, a particular way of encoding, decoding and recoding things. The key to that process is value: valuation, valorization, capital as the vehicle for the valuation and valorization of capital. In the theorization of money offered in *Capitalism and Schizophrenia*, it is finance – the operation of financing, and then of valuing things according to financial standards – that endows the capitalistic signification apparatus with its defining features. So, then, is this regime of signs of a properly schizophrenic nature? Is capital psychotic? There is no straightforward answer to that question in those pages, nor a frontal examination of the specifics of financial valuation and their paranoid potentials. But the project is there, ready to be confronted.

There is a trap in that project, though. The trap of hastily conflating finance and madness. Who has not read repeatedly about markets gone crazy? About manic traders and investors in panic? About finance being made of delusion? The tropes of mad finance are certainly found everywhere. Narratives of financial insanity abound in mass media accounts, often conveying the idea of the spuriousness and whimsicality of representation in financial markets. They also populate the pages of the scholarly critique of finance, where the vocabulary of mental disorder and behavioral irrationality finds a significant place. And they certainly feature in mainstream doctrines of financial management, for which the trouble with finance – i.e., "crisis" – ought to be solved through recourse to a sane, rational, responsible, realist, intelligent, healthy appraisal of value.

But the idea of rationality in finance is part of the trouble, and so is the concomitant idea of financial irrationality. Thus understood, the conflation of finance and madness represents in fact quite a meager understanding of psychotic logic.

Schizophrenia is, by all cogent accounts, a disease of rationality. It is characterized, most saliently, by an obsessive sense of rational inquiry, an excess of interpretation, a fixation with the logic of things, a compulsion to decode, and a radical search for the ultimate foundation of everything. It is a spiraling search, full of pain and despair. But it has rationality – overabundant – at its core. It is the rationality of finance, and not the lack of it, that can evolve toward a delirious form. Signaling a delusional periphery at the margins of financial sanity means missing the prodromal syndrome that lies at its heart.

And what is this financial rationality about, then? Accounts of finance as madness typically focus on the stereotype of "speculative value." That is, of a value given by the market solely on the grounds of the anticipation of that market value. The trouble with finance would then be caused by a delusional reliance on virtual, fictitious, immediate value, and an incapacity to refer to a real economy where fundamental, veracious, long-standing value is to be found. Finance is then considered as a mirage. A mirage that would make sense, as such, against the benchmark of something that would not: the palpable, concrete value of productive investment. But this is a mistake. This is a truncated picture of finance: one that neglects the core of financial imagination.

Speculative value is certainly part of the language of finance. But so is "fundamental value." This notion is at the center of the myriad guidelines and textbooks that form the financial mind. Asset managers and financial analysts use it routinely. In his ethnographic account of mundane valuation practices in investment banks, Horacio Ortiz (2014, 2021) observes the tensions at work between what finance professionals themselves call speculative value and fundamental value. The speculative value of an asset refers to the market, to its moods and fancies, and to the prices that are formed there. The fundamental value, in turn, resides in the asset's power to generate a return in the future. It is the value of investing in that asset, and it demands calculation: it is about gauging that prospective yield while assessing its likelihood. When finance professionals speak of an asset being "overvalued" or "undervalued," they explicitly mean that the market price – speculative value – does not reflect correctly the actual worth – fundamental value – of that asset. Finance thus relies on a critique of speculative value. Yet it is a paradoxical critique, grounded as it is on the idea that markets can eventually correct and end up reflecting fundamental value efficiently.

Here, perhaps, lies the prime trouble with financial imagination. The financial industry, a gigantic structure within which the power to make money with money is organized, is controlled by a justification template at the center of which operates a vernacular notion of value. Of true value and false value. Of true value that is said to derive from the future, to be created on the basis of rational valuation standards, to be assessed against the odds of uncertainty. And of false value originating in short-term speculation, in the wobbly standards of market opinion, and in the thrill of gambling. Two kinds of value that can morph into each other: sometimes auspiciously, as when market opinion is correctly informed and successfully reflects the fundamental value of things; fatally some other times, as when risk assessment is corrupted by the excesses of market fads. When finance professionals speak of crisis they mean precisely this: a crack in valuation, with market prices not making sense to investors who cannot appraise the proper value of things anymore.

So financial imagination is entirely about that. It is about investors estimating the fundamental value of things, meeting in the market to express their valuation and freely interacting accordingly. It is about money being wisely allocated in order to create value, which means making money with money, but in a virtuous, veracious fashion, since that value creation is what allows society to thrive. It is about making sense of the disruption of that process in the terms of a crisis of valuation, a crisis in which the market is no longer able to express the true value of things, with investors losing confidence, liquidity being lost and the flow of money drying out, unable to irrigate the economy, unable to fecundate it, unable to create more value. When the critique of finance is articulated in the terms of protecting fundamental value from the perils of speculative value, of defending real value creation against the malevolent dissipation of value, it is located within the perimeter of financial imagination, not outside of it.

The moral ascendancy of finance is particularly noticeable when its vocabulary extends its metaphorical grip. The jargon of value creation recurrently moves to the terrain of social problems, for example, with virtuous financiers and caring entrepreneurs exerting their investment gaze in order to fulfill the promise of social impact. A pragmatic ductility – if not indeterminacy – of the notion of value is found at work there, as Emily Barman (2016) notes. Making money and doing good become the same. More than that: making money guarantees the very possibility of doing good. It is not so much that there are conflicting values, with some being financial and some others being moral. Finance is one type of moral discourse. It is rather that the very notion of value (including so-called social value) works as an effective metaphor that unleashes the potentials of the idea of virtuous reality being the outcome of a will to invest.

Financial imagination is in fact packed with metaphors. The metaphor of value creation is perhaps the most insidious one, and perhaps also the most operative and consequential. Operative and consequential: metaphors are indeed taken here from the standpoint of their institutive capacity. They open spaces of signification, they serve as vehicles for realization, they operate as cognitive instruments, providing clarity and obscurity at once. Their generative power needs to be considered with the precaution advocated throughout the philosophical scrutiny of this semiotic engine (Blumenberg 2010; Eco 1983; Ricœur 1977). And the generative power of the metaphor of value creation – for this is a metaphor indeed – certainly demands precaution. By its virtue, the act of making money with money amounts to the creation of a substance – value – that flows within the economy, making it flourish. But, in order for this to happen, protection is required: protection from the ills of a vile and vicious use of money that, instead of creating value, destroys it.

Metaphors control the foundations of political economy. Metaphors of good value and bad value indeed sustain doctrines of economics throughout their history, disseminating within them their semiotic traction. And that traction is often of a spiritual kind. In his investigations on the religious – Western Christian – origins of the categories of modern economics, Giacomo Todeschini (2009, 2021) signals the grip exerted by metaphors of bodily health and circulating fluids, but also by stereotypical representations of the carriers of economic disease. These are certainly most recognizable in myths and fantasies surrounding Jews and Judaism: unruly hoarding, financial cruelty, poisonous credit, cryptic interest, disregard for salvation and other variations on the antisemitic repertoire, as other historians contribute to demonstrating (Trivellato 2019). And this is of relevance for the examination of the contours of financial imagination today. The very idea of value creation requires in fact, in order just to make sense, the positing of a symmetrical idea of value destruction: something against which to delineate, and protect, the wonder of veritable value. The idea of the enemies of value and its cohort of invasive metaphors become therefore structurally necessary, the antisemitic repertoire providing here a prototypical resource.

The antisemitic syndrome is certainly manifold, sometimes enrooted in racial figurations or religious traditions, some other times adopting a more abstract or elusive outlook. In most of its instances – although perhaps more effectively in its more abstracting versions – the antisemitic syndrome carries an element of economic fetishism. This is about locating in finance capital the sign of a devious inclination, perhaps linked to a specific human type, parasitic and cruel in nature, that endangers the truth and virtue of value creation. The argument put forward by Moishe Postone (1980) in his assessment of the antisemitic kernel of National Socialism is illuminating in this respect. The key to the understanding of Nazi Germany is, he suggests, a theory of value: a widespread vernacular theory of value creation and value destruction for which the critique of capitalism consists, in fact, in the glorification of a kind of capitalism dubbed natural, healthy, organic, patrimonial and native, against the ills caused by the infectious, rootless agents of false, speculative value. What needs to be addressed is not only the incongruity of these views. The point is also to understand their phantasmal power.

For there is power in the fantasies of value creation: the power of metaphors that can foster hopes and fears, creating orientation and disorientation at once. At the center of this semiotic engine lies the most precious and fragile of all ingredients: time. The tale of a linear, promissory time at the end of which one will be able to collect one's return, provided that the uncertainties surrounding the yield are safely navigated in the present. There is obviously a salvific, redemptory element in the way the future is envisioned in financial culture. This is a fact that has been aptly established in the tradition of the historical sociology of capitalism represented by Max Weber. But there is more to it than that. It is not only that financial capitalism requires an idea of time loaded with the justification of a spiritual entitlement to the productivity of money. It is that the very idea of time in which capital operates is in fact an idea of time as capital: an artifact, altogether, of financial imagination.

Time often features as the medium in which the meaning of capital operates, with ideals of value stemming from prospective, future yield and requiring, accordingly, careful assessment of what is termed "risk" in financial parlance. But, as Éric Alliez (1996) contributes to showing, it is the semiotic operation of capital that produces that particular concept of time, a concept of abstract time considered, then, in the terms of monetary investment. Alliez further refines that argument, claiming precisely that this semiotic operation requires the invention of a space of non-value from which society (a society busy with value and whose time shall be devoted to the production thereof) should be separated and protected. But that society, thus configured, is enmeshed within the tensions that this elusive notion of time prompts. This viewpoint is in direct, explicit connection with the project sketched out in *Capitalism and Schizophrenia* (Deleuze and Guattari 1983, 1987). It is about locating within the fabric of financial imagination the trouble of a radicalized (and radicalizing) idea of time.

This radicalized idea of time is most visibly at work within the conflicts and contradictions that constitute prevailing financial culture today. In her remarkable examination of the defining qualities of predominant valuation methodologies, Liliana Doganova (2024) shows how inherently paradoxical the notion of future value is. That notion – a political technology, she writes – entails thinking as an investor and perceiving in today's strategic decisions the reflection of future flows. But it also requires pricing accordingly the courage to invest, which means reassessing those future flows in the light of the risk represented by time, confiscating not only the present but also that imagined future, which needs accordingly to undergo a process of devaluation. This is certainly not madness – quite the contrary. It constitutes the dominant rationality of capital budgeting, business strategy and economic policy today. But it contains a paradox: a tension that lives in the loopholes of financial imagination.

There is a consistent case, it seems, for the idea possibly lurking beneath the surface of *Capitalism and Schizophrenia*. This is the idea of a troubled regime of signs inherent in financial imagination. Paranoid finance, then, but not in the sense of some sort of a financial madness that would haunt the edifice of normal economic sanity. Paranoid finance rather in the sense of a constitutive potential lodged in the mundane, naturalized notion of value creation that operates at the center of financial imagination today. With the very concept of value considered as the prodromal syndrome of an always possible, and incessantly approaching, semiotic debacle: one excited by a too expressive, too explicit, too radical, too hopeful faith. This semiotic debacle is then about some sort of a value panic, akin to the agency panic that Timothy Melley (2000) identifies in paranoid culture: an intense anxiety about the forces that shape, control, unleash or confiscate "value" (whatever this phantasmal and elusive notion may refer to).

A radicalization of value

Value features recurrently in conspiratorial discourse. It features there in multiple guises, although almost always tainted with some kind of moral radicalism. Money, finance, capital, wealth and profit populate, indeed, the visions of hope and despair typically found in conspiratorial ideation, often in combination with elements of cultic, millennialist, esoteric or paranormal belief. But they do so in reference to a critical compass: one that allows telling good value from bad value, and true value from false value. A compass which, inadvertently or not, exacerbates the troubles of financial imagination. Narratives of false value abound, which signal money as the ultimate driver of the evil forces that control society.

Dubious genealogies and monstrous inclinations are identified within the banking industry, and the capitalist elite is irrevocably associated with a sense of fakeness and falsehood. Narratives of true value are opposed to this, with salvation acquiring the contours of emancipation from economic servitude. Alternatives to the financial order are discovered, often in the form of access to redemptory currencies, and to the radical restoration of the veritable foundations of value.

The QAnon syndrome offers perhaps a most vivid illustration of this. QAnon is best understood as a multifaceted assemblage of conspiratorial narratives, combining intense spiritual elements and translating into a patchy cluster of extremist, populist political movements (Bloom and Moskalenko 2021; Gulyas 2021; Rothschild 2021; Sommer 2023). It emerged in the late 2010s in North America, and its roots are to be found in the particular improvisational blend of millennialism, conspiratorialism and libertarianism identified by scholars of spiritual and political culture in the United States (Barkun 2003; Crockford 2021; Fenster 2008; Knight 2000; Konda 2019; Melley 2000; Robertson 2016). It gained endemic political relevance and global reach in the early 2020s, and morphed into numerous variations, combinations and deviations. The QAnon tag fails, in fact, to cover the manifold reality it refers to, parts of which may be better recognized through other markers: the so-called sovereign citizen movement, or the radical right, or the idea of a "New World Order" or of a "Great Awakening," for example. It effectively points, though, toward the centrality of financial value within the conspiratorial fantasy.

Mike Rothschild (2021) and Aaron John Gulyas (2021), among others, document the centrality of the financial element in QAnon. There is an enemy in the QAnon narrative, and that enemy has to do with money. It is an enemy of true value, portrayed in the form of a globalist elite, a mixture of bankers, artists and politicians forming an immoral, parasitic scheme. Metaphors abound that convey the idea of a fluid of primordial value that would be confiscated and then absorbed by this enemy. This is an image loaded with antisemitic tropes and representations of moral cruelty – such as satanic ritual abuse of children – quite obviously connected to the blood libel and other antisemitic myths (Teter 2020). There is an obsession with the global financial power of the Rothschild family and of George Soros, also the Rockefeller family and Bill Gates, and a fixation with the toxic power of the Federal Reserve System of the United States, and of intergovernmental organizations that are said to serve the purpose of instituting global control, such as the United Nations.

A pattern is discernible, akin to the figuration of a precious treasure of fundamental value that is compromised, sequestered and devastated by the evil agents of speculative value. This is abstract enough to admit different concrete instantiations, at times succumbing to spiritual obsession or sexual imagination (e.g., a fixation with pedophilia and the elixir of youth), at times more attuned to a critique of the banking industry and a preoccupation with valuation, indebtedness, taxation and economic regulation. But the financial template of these conspiratorial fantasies is perhaps more tractable if one considers how deliverance from such evils is envisioned. QAnon is about menace, but also about liberation and triumph. It is about a combination of popular uprising, secret war and astute anticipation that will overturn the order of false value. And the financial element becomes critical there.

References to NESARA/GESARA surface when one searches for immediate precedents and influences within the QAnon syndrome (Gulyas 2021; Rothschild 2021). NESARA, an intriguing acronym, stood initially for National Economic Stabilization and Recovery Act. This referred to a rather fringe and unconventional economic policy proposal ideated in the 1990s by Harvey F. Barnard, a consultant and founder of a NESARA Institute established in Greenwell Springs, Louisiana. The initiative, which took the form of a proposed bill but was never introduced before the US Congress, consisted in a systematic monetary and fiscal reform aiming at "draining the swamp" and establishing "general prosperity" (against the "contrived scheme" put in place by "power brokers in Washington, DC"). This included things such as the restoration of gold as constitutional currency, the end of the Federal Reserve System, the elimination of national debt, the abolition of compound interest on loans, and of income tax.

The 2000s saw the acronym evolve, now standing for National Economic Security and Reformation Act and referring to a rather esoteric version of the plan, soon acquiring a planetary dimension, in the form of a Global Economic Security and Reformation Act, GESARA. Shaini Goodwin – a spirituality and investment consultant known as the "Dove of Oneness" in New Age internet circles – spearheaded this new conspiratorial interpretation. The "global currency reset" and the general "revaluation" the reform called for were considered to be in fact under way, although in a secret, occulted fashion, with an adverse league of political and financial elites conspiring against the changes. NESARA/GESARA also started to carry a distinctive spiritual, prophetic element, with the restoration of the fair, original, real value of persons and things being connected to the equilibrium of energies – at once planetary, cosmic, mystical, psychic, extra-terrestrial, interdimensional, divine and economic.

Myriad NESARA/GESARA groups, seminars, conferences, publications and tutorials exist today, in the early 2020s, all over the world. Investigative reporting from the BBC and Bellingcat demonstrates the breadth of the phenomenon (Griffin and Sardarizadeh 2021; Mossou and Geiger 2022). Firsthand accounts provide a remarkable wealth of details on the webs of hope, fraud, legend and disarray that the NESARA/GESARA syndrome is made of: from online shops in which one can purchase cheap Iraqi dinar or Vietnamese dong in anticipation of the imminent NESARA/GESARA rollout (and then make a fortune when the time comes), to convoluted revelations about the functioning of the "Quantum Financial System" (the nexus of banking software and hardware that sustains the NESARA/GESARA project), the secret war between the Alliance (a global confederation striving to implement the reform) and the Cabal (the corrupt defenders of the old financial order), the crucial role played by the Chinese Elders of the Royal Dragon (a set of ancient families working covertly for the restoration of the gold standard), and much more. It is an elaborate fantasy quite attuned to a QAnon worldview, cluttered with elements of conspiratorial thinking, mixtures of antisemitic tropes and spiritual visions, and also ideals of political reform and economic salvation.

This is then certainly about economic salvation, a vision at whose heart lies, indeed, a vernacular theory of value: a theory of the confiscation of real value, supplemented with a theory of the restoration thereof by means of a prodigious reform.

A prodigious, fantastic currency, more exactly. In her examination of the cosmologies of money found in North American communities of spiritual investment practice, Susannah Crockford (2022) addresses explicitly the fantasized properties of gold found in NESARA/GESARA theorizations of the gold standard. Discourse on the properties of currency – of any form of currency, be it gold or otherwise – is generally far from immune to fantasizing, though. This is certainly a lesson learned from an anthropological perspective, which habitually notices the mystical element at work in the cultural conventions that sustain any attempt at making sense of currency. Nigel Dodd (2014) convincingly maps the cracks and loopholes that beset any attempt at establishing a univocal foundation for the value of money. The trouble is not with fantasy, then. The trouble is with the radicalization of fantasy – the fantasy not only of a univocal foundation for the value of money, but also, more fatally, of an extreme vision of how that univocal foundation determines everything else.

The elements of value radicalism found in the NESARA/GESARA syndrome and in adjacent QAnon variations can be recognized in other contemporaneous threads. Bitcoin comes to mind quite naturally. Bitcoin and, more generally, the surge in digital distributed transaction encryption technologies that gained worldwide momentum in the 2010s and were quick to be presented in the terms of – decentralized, emancipatory, liberal, alternative, revolutionary – currencies. David Golumbia (2016) pertinently establishes the extremist, conspiratorial lineage that informs the political discourse at work in both the inception and the use of such instruments. The similarities with NESARA/GESARA narratives are striking. It is true that so-called cryptocurrencies may very well be approached through the angle of sheer technicality alone. They can also be effectively examined from the perspective of fraud, damage, cult and delusion (Faux 2023; Gerard 2017; Howson 2023; McKenzie and Silverman 2023). But they also exemplify a radicalization of financial imagination. Bitcoin conveys, at least in part, the idea of a world that would at last resemble the outcome of a perfect flow of free investors transacting freely, freely reclaiming their own legitimate value, and freely organizing their existence – and everything else – accordingly.

Bitcoin is quite tangibly embedded within an atmosphere of exhilaration and disinhibition. The same goes for so-called decentralized finance in general. This is quite visible in the surreal expressions of thrill, rapture and excess – "power to the people," "start the fire," "open your mind" – documented in firsthand accounts, as investigative reporting from Bloomberg manifestly shows (Goldman 2022). This is even more noticeable when these cultures permeate aesthetic expression and the art market. Methods for the distributed encryption of ownership certification in the exchange of digital files – so-called non-fungible tokens – prompted in the late 2010s a remarkable effervescence in the artistic figuration of stereotypical, shallow icons in digital format: expressive forms in which one could easily recognize the atmosphere of exhilaration and disinhibition (and also perhaps of silliness) found in cryptocurrency circles. A key, again, for the interpretation of this cultural orientation is a radicalization of financial imagination, and of the idea of value that is inherent in it. In her incisive critique of this movement in the art industry, Geraldine Juárez (2021, 2022) explicitly observes how the whole point of these novel forms of artistic creativity and exchange is to consider art – everything in art, from artwork to artist, to art public too – in terms of asset management, and to do so in the most radical manner possible.

The critique of finance, again, finds itself controlled by the stereotypes of value that constitute financial imagination as such. Hopes of unrestrained revaluation draw from aspirations to individual sovereignty: the sovereignty of an investing self that ought to navigate unreservedly a landscape of value signs, and escape the malicious control of centralizing institutions, state apparatuses and contrived monopolies. And this, again, precipitates spiraling interpretations of who to side with and who to fight against. The paranoid element sparks up, in turn. This is, again, about protecting from depredation a value that is deemed fundamental but is in fact nowhere to be found – it is a chimera – and about reproducing indeed, magnified and distorted, the very character of depredation. The figment of a magical currency fits into narratives of radical freedom, which is indeed best understood as the radical freedom of value itself. And this is all the more effective when embedded into a narrative of crisis. Or into a reality of crisis interpreted within the narrative of finance – i.e., a crisis of fundamental valuation.

Scholars of contemporary conspiratorial thought signal the resurgence of so-called sovereign citizen movements in the wake of the financial crisis of 2008 (Hodge 2019). The context is most significant. The troubles that quite distinctively characterized the credit crisis that affected a large portion of developed economies in the late 2000s and early 2010s steered the formation of a political critique of finance that got manifestly stuck in the industry's lingo of liquidity, solvency, risk and valuation (Langley 2015). Diffuse, anticipatory anxiety intensified in the everyday experience of investment and debt (Deville 2015; Komporozos-Athanasiou 2022). Value became a semiotic stronghold for institutional reformation and populist confrontation alike. The crisis had been caused, the dominant narrative went, by the faulty and malign appraisal of the real value of all kinds of assets. The response ought to reside, accordingly, in the restoration of some sort of a trustworthy and transparent valuation process. And it could lead also, more radically, to a redemptory plan, at the end of which the true value of everything – especially of oneself, considered as investor in one's own life – could be regained and reclaimed.

This is one important thread in the ideological kernel of sovereign citizen movements. The loose ensemble of collectives and doctrines that go by that name – and which certainly links to the QAnon syndrome on many grounds – finds most of its recognized antecedents in the North American radical right, particularly in anti-government militia varieties. It is nurtured, more generally, by ideals of freedom and truth that are well entrenched in North American traditions of extremist libertarianism and religious millennialism. It is marked by an aversion to state authority and to any form of taxation, and by a critique of the banking industry that is often tainted with antisemitic elements. It is likewise characterized by a sanctification of private property, and by a fixation with the constitutional aspects of the North American legal system. And it is generally grounded on a sense of religious spirituality, usually of the Christian kind. But these elements do not preclude sovereign citizen movements from adopting idiosyncratic forms, morphing into novel variations, or combining with other traditions, in the United States, Canada and Australia, but also elsewhere in the world, particularly in the United Kingdom and in Continental Europe, and in Latin America, Asia and Africa too.

The sovereign citizen syndrome is usually detectable in expressions of repudiation of established legal order and government authority. The state apparatus, deemed corrupted by the private interests of a world elite, is no longer recognized as a depository of legitimate power. This translates, for example, into the refusal to comply with fiscal policy or license regulation. Such vision applies to the banking industry too, with the rejection of debt payment on the grounds that established financial duties no longer apply once one has reclaimed one's own contractual sovereignty. Access to secret, alternative forms of wealth features often as part of the narrative – as in NESARA/GESARA. The conspiratorial element is pervasive, tax avoidance and investment advice being wrapped into sometimes highly esoteric fantasies of personal freedom and global machination.

Both delusion and radicalization are necessarily highlighted in the analysis of this phenomenon. Christine Sarteschi (2020, 2021) documents extensively the confrontational views and practices developed in sovereign citizen milieus, and the psychological disarray these may come with. The paranoid element warrants a psychoanalytical perspective as well (Matheson 2018). Investigative reporting, from Vice News for example (Hines 2021; Lamoureux 2022), has documented the obsession with child custody and war rhetoric. But it is perhaps the legal dimension that has attracted more scholarly attention. Law scholars have extensively documented – with palpable perplexity and recurrent use of notions of madness – the rise of "pseudolaw" in these movements (Barrows 2021; Griffin 2022; Harris 2005; Levin and Mitchell 1999; McRoberts 2019; Netolitzky 2018, 2019, 2021; Weir 2015). This term refers to forms of vernacular legal knowledge developed by practitioners, conducive to the purported rebuttal of recognized legal authority and the establishment of a new legal order. It is characterized by the use of an original vocabulary: a quite surprising semiotic regime that subverts conventional terminology while mirroring a savant style in legal parlance. This often translates into burdensome and disruptive litigation – so-called "paper terrorism" – and into disappointment, especially for "pseudolitigants" themselves.

There is a cultic, magic component to sovereign citizen discourse that should not be neglected. This is most visible in the perception of the power of legal ceremony and vocabulary, and in the quite fetishistic properties attributed to written documents, to typographic emphasis (under-lining, bolding, capitalization, italicization), to ink signatures and thumbprints, to declamatory assertions and to legalistic symbols. Donald J. Netolitzky (2018, 2019, 2021) explicitly indicates this analytical direction, drawing from extensive documentation of pseudolegal litigation, and also from experience gathered from legal counseling with the superior trial court of the province of Alberta in Canada. The pseudolegal argument, he contributes to show, depends on a fantasized hierarchy of legal systems, in which a superior and primordial jurisdiction of so-called natural or common law – the law of the natural world, considered as a divine creation, and of sponta-neous contracts between free human beings – supersedes all other legal rules and authorities. These inferior rules and authorities are critiqued on the grounds of their contrived, fictitious char-acter. For example, claims about the usual notion of the legal person being a fiction abound in sovereign citizen milieus: one should dissociate from one's legal name, as it represents the ascendancy of some malevolent legal order – corporate law, commercial law – in the determination of who one is. This view is known as the "strawman theory" in conspiratorial thought: one's name, the one written in one's birth certificate, is an artifact of governmental control. In a taxation court case, for example, litigants ought to clearly repudiate the name with which the judge is addressing them.

The cultic, magic component is conveyed remarkably well through the semiotic inventiveness of the legalistic syntax used in such milieus, starting with the so-called "quantum grammar" developed by David Wynn Miller, a legal consultant and key theorist in the North American sovereign citizen environment (Barrows 2021; Griffin 2022; McRoberts 2019; Netolitzky 2018, 2019; Sarteschi 2020, 2021). This is a set of syntactical and interpretive precepts and formularies that are meant to deliver a "correct language" capable not only of referring unambiguously to the entities under consideration, but also of enacting them firmly and irrevocably. It can be easily recognized through a series of markers: effusive punctuation, convoluted vocabulary, recurrent parsing, but also a sense of litany and invocation, if not of incantation. It seems to be based on the idea that words possess an energy (literally) whose correct channeling enhances the performative efficacy of language, connecting indeed to ideas popular in quantum mysticism (Burwell 2013). To this is added the habitual recourse to etymological fantasies in sovereign citizen talk, such as when litigants refuse to acknowledge that they "understand" the claims or questions addressed by the judge, because "to understand" means to them literally "to stand under" and therefore surrendering one's legal capacity. Unlocking the covert force of words means recoding the power of the law.

The crux in this cultic, magic component is value, though. It is about unlocking the secrets of value. It is about pseudolaw, but it is also about "pseudofinance" and "pseudobanking," so to speak. The sovereign citizen world is, to quite an extent, a world of financial scheme promoters. As in the case of NESARA/GESARA, varieties of the sovereign citizen movement have to do with access to secret knowledge about the functioning of the banking system, and about fabulous techniques for debt relief, asset management and infinite wealth. References to quantum grammar feature, tortuously, in firsthand interpretations of the advent of the Quantum Financial System (a crucial element of NESARA/GESARA narratives). Also, more generally, the strawman theory that underpins sovereign citizen discourse is deeply entrenched within a conspiratorial fantasy of money, banking, finance and value at large. One fundamental vehicle of value resides here in the birth certificate – that is, the document that derives from the registration of one's existence within a dedicated government office and which represents, it is implied, one's value as a human being. But the birth certificate is in fact, precisely, a sequestration of that value by a machinery of surreptitious enslavement. The aim is, the narrative goes, to reclaim and liberate that value.

This syndrome is perhaps best exemplified by a sovereign citizen derivative traceable through the acronym "OPPT" – sometimes "OPPT 1776," in reference to the year of the declaration of independence of the United States. It stands for "One People's Public Trust" and it refers originally to a particular scheme: a legal, financial technique invented by a small group of people in 2012 in the

United States. It also refers to a wider movement. Communities of OPPT practitioners developed first in the United States, Canada, Australia and then elsewhere, in Europe (especially Austria, Germany, Italy, also the United Kingdom, Spain, France) and Latin America (Argentina, Chile). Despite the loss of momentum of the original initiative, it gained strong international traction in 2020 and 2021, in part due to reactions to policy measures prompted by the global COVID-19 epidemic, but also because it offered a set of precepts and explanations that handily bridged together elements of the strawman theory, of "New World Order" and "Great Awakening" conspiratorial narratives, of New Age spirituality and quantum mysticism, and of financial hope (also including, sometimes, QAnon, Illuminati, Reptilians and Ascended Masters, and some other times cryptocurrencies and financial arbitrage).

OPPT's complex, evolving set of precepts and explanations revolves around two principal ideas. The first idea is the discovery of the fact that governments are in fact private corporations, parties to a malignant trust, which use their subjected citizens – their birth certificates – as collateral in order to access money in the global financial system, depriving them of their natural right to access their own value. The second idea is that this state of bondage can be broken though the writing and filing of a series of complicated legal documents that constitute a renewed universal trust, confirm the foreclosure of all governments, declare one's lawful individual sovereignty, and release access to unlimited money corresponding to one's essential value. These two supposed insights are recognizable in other sovereign citizen strains. But in the OPPT syndrome they acquire a rather sophisticated level of intellectual elaboration and practical formalization. And this is particularly the case for the theory of value – and value creation – inherent in it.

Heather Ann Tucci-Jarraf, early OPPT initiator and the movement's spiritual reference, sketches out in her declarations a theory of value in which a mystical, demiurgic ideal of value is connected to the functioning of the banking system. She talks about the soul as an eternal asset, about people not only being the origin of value but being value proper, and then about the entitlement to regaining ownership of that unlimited value through the banking circuit, establishing each living human being as a "Creator's Value

Asset Center" (CVAC). The ultimate currency, the one that represents the fundamental value of the eternal essence, is oneself – oneself duly uttering "I am" – or rather everyone – the "we is" or "we is I am," as she says, the purposeful grammar error vindicating here the restoration of the value of a "one people" or a "one nation" of some sort. She envisions and promises a "Universal Value Exchange" which operates accounts in that currency and allows access to infinite flows of value (for details, see Appendix).

Formerly a practicing lawyer (a law graduate with experience in litigation, and additional training in accounting and finance), Tucci-Jarraf gained prominence in sovereign citizen milieus in the early 2010s when she started developing, together with a small group of acolytes, a kind of intricate method for financial emancipation roughly based on an elaboration of the strawman theory (Barrows 2021; Netolitzky 2019; Sarteschi 2020). The method revolved around the careful filing of UCC documents: UCC stands for the Uniform Commercial Code, a body of norms that govern the regulation of commercial transactions within and across states in the United States. The promise was that this ought to result in the access to unlimited amounts of money: first, through the establishment of a legal trust by virtue of which the foreclosure of all banks, all states and all corporations is ratified; then, through the declaration of one's personal sovereignty as a living human soul; next, through the sheer reclamation of the value due to oneself on account of that; and, finally, through the articulation of legal immunity in the face of any adverse situation.

The initiative evolved into a network of advocates and practitioners, first in the United States, then elsewhere as part of a "global tour" in 2013 (which included a move toward additional interests, for example on inventions for the production of free energy), which partly established itself in 2014 as a community (which fell apart shortly after, it seems) in the province of Tétouan, Morocco. Tucci-Jarraf was arrested in 2017 on charges of bank and wire fraud, together with associate Randall Keith Beane, who had initially presented her as his lawyer. Her arrest took place outside the White House in Washington, DC, apparently, after agents from the Federal Bureau of Investigation got a tip that she was demanding to meet with President Donald Trump. Both

Tucci-Jarraf and Beane were tried in 2018 in Knoxville, Tennessee. Tucci-Jarraf was sentenced to 4 years and 9 months in prison for conspiring to launder money.

The OPPT syndrome took a quite different path from 2018 onward. Its ties to the original group of initiators and advocates waned. It morphed into an unstructured complex of loosely interconnected advocates and apprentices that were trying to learn about the OPPT doctrine, studying the original OPPT 1776 UCC filings and declarations, examining the tutorials that had been left scattered over the internet, sharing insights, reinterpreting all this in the light of other theories and traditions. Online video seminars and presentations flourished in the early 2020s, in different languages and with different orientations, and numerous websites started offering guidance in OPPT matters – in English, Spanish, Italian, French or German. A video posted by a popular specialist in 2021 on an internet platform could easily register tens of thousands of views and hundreds of comments. This flow of OPPT materials combined sometimes with quite disparate elements: from esotericism and mysticism to alternative medicine and astrology, from nationalism and populism to cryptocurrency and investment advice. OPPT watchwords are found, for example, in the rhetoric of the Reichsbürger movement in Germany and in other extremist formations of the populist, radical right in the world. But they can be found too in cultic movements whose main claims to sovereignty are of a spiritual, naturopathic type. Testimonials abound on internet platforms of people trying to make sense of the method, attempting to do some of the paperwork, promoting this as a component of a secessionist project or an extremist plot, or just using it as a lever to express freedom and happiness – or to make friends and eventually some free money (see Appendix).

All these kinds of discourse bear the mark of derangement. They are imbued with conspiratorial fanaticism in some cases, with delusional spiritualism or with libertarian extremism in other cases, but there is in all of them – and in many other comparable strains – an element of spiraling interpretation, foundational dream and paranoid thought. And in all there is a fixation with value: value of the bad kind and of the good kind, false value and true value, false value to be exposed and contested, true value to be unlocked and reclaimed. A hope for a system of signs that would allow for the lasting, truthful representation and exchange of the value of things. A radicalization of value, then: a paranoid regime of signs that carries the trouble of financial imagination.

Tensions within the mainstream

The narrative of paranoid finance offers, in part, a reconstruction of problems that are inherent in the paradoxes of economic value. It is a delirious reconstruction. But it is a reconstruction of something – the economic mainstream – that is already slightly delirious, loaded as it is with metaphors of good and evil, with references to the impenetrable foundations of true value, and with admonitions against the agents of false value. It is a narrative that works within the boundaries of financial imagination – an imagination of free investors writing contracts and maximizing their value – inadvertently exposing the delusion that these boundaries generate. The economic mainstream is not the antidote to paranoid finance, but rather the cluster of worldviews that nurtures it. It contains the residue of the unsettled tensions carried by the very idea of value.

The economic mainstream inherits heavily, in this respect, from the tradition of political economy. And the tradition of political economy is cluttered with disquisitions on the foundations of value. Concepts of value are indeed deeply entrenched within the scientific and normative narratives of political economy (Pitts 2021). An abundant number of such narratives are about signaling contradictions between one particular economic process and what its inherent value is or should be about – or, on the contrary, about demonstrating that value is reflected perfectly within that particular economic process. And this is what political economy was and is about, classical and neoclassical alike, before and after it morphed into the calculative science of economics. From François Quesnay to Adam Smith, David Ricardo or Karl Marx, from Léon Walras to William Stanley Jevons and Alfred Marshall, and then to Joseph Schumpeter, John Maynard Keynes or Irving Fisher, the intellectual effort is tangibly about coming up with an ultimate source of economic value, be it land, labor, exchange, opinion, time, capital, knowledge or some-thing else. And about dreaming of a society that would abide by that benchmark. The ductility and incompleteness of Marx's evolving thought, caught as it was between political economy and the critique thereof, represents a landmark rather than a turning point in these narratives.

It has sometimes been argued that value is no longer an important keyword in contemporary economics, having faded into the vocabulary of utility, cost, discount, expectation or price. But this is hardly true, for all these concepts always contain a justificatory charge. An idea of value is always at work when a price, for example, is justi-fied or criticized (Boltanski and Esquerre 2020). If a price is said not to look good, it is because it is considered that it does not represent value well. And the economic mainstream is certainly not immune to talk about crashes and bubbles, about assets being underpriced or overpriced. This is precisely the point: what is meant when claims are made about something being wrong with a price is that that price has failed in represent-ing accurately the actual, real value of the thing under consideration. And the same goes with the bundle of contemporary obsessions about how to better value the future, whatever that means (Doganova 2024). These are about exercising a theory of value, purposefully or inadvertently.

How is that a problem? It makes perfect sense to say that things have value. And it sounds quite reasonable to claim that that value comes from somewhere. And, once this foundation is settled, it seems perfectly acceptable to think that value can be then reflected wrongly or rightly. But value is invisible. And being at once true and invisible is not a comfortable state to be in. It is vital not to neglect how irrepressible this notion can become, and how its meaning can escalate into an extreme principle, haunted at the same time by its interpretive power and by its intrinsic hollowness. True and invisible, indeed: just like gods are supposed to be.

In the pages he devotes to the problem of the analysis of wealth in political economy, Michel Foucault (1970) hints at one of the reasons why a regime of representational truth does not suit economic value particularly well. The medium for the representation of economic value is money, but money is also what is represented. The sign that refers to wealth is already wealth. The puzzles that this representational loop generates are recorded in a long cultural tradition that interrogates the theatrical aspects of the representation of value in the marketplace, and the dissociation of sign from thing that this representation entails (Agnew 1986; Shell 1982). This puzzle is intrinsically linked to one of the most remarkable properties of money: that of being abstractive (Ingham 2004). Money requires a notion of value – the value of money – in order to operate, but its operation consists primarily in abstracting that value. Money thus contains a contradiction: it is at once wealth and a fantasy of wealth (Dodd 2014). And this contradiction is, at the same time, intrinsically irreducible from a theoretical perspective and unceasingly reduced in mundane, practical experience. A mystery. Overwhelming if one insists on focusing on solving it; trivial if one does not take it too seriously and just carries on.

The mystery holds, in part, because it contains a theological element. The Western Christian tradition is packed with tropes of divine power and tropes of monetary currency that feed mutually, as Devin Singh (2018) cogently shows. The metaphor of the "coin of god" is particularly crucial here. Christ as the coin of god. Humankind, more generally, as the coin of god. The value of the human soul as the product of heavenly minting. The parallel between the shape of the holy host and that of a good coin, and between salvation and investment. These are commonplace tropes in medieval economic thought, as indicated also by Giacomo Todeschini (2009), among others. Their theological origins, however, do more than provide economic existence with a spiritual layer. The metaphor of the coin of god feeds directly an idea that is perhaps best expressed in the jargon of paranoid finance: that of value being the intrinsic substance of the human soul, divinely imprinted, sacred. Invisible, but sacred and true. The Christian element is indeed palpable in many of the conspiratorial, millennialist varieties that exemplify a radicalization of financial imagination. The magic gold currency in NESARA/ GESARA, the self as a Creator's Value Asset Center in OPPT, and so forth, not to mention the QAnon fixation with priceless children falling into the tenebrous hands of the enemies of value.

Does the mystery of money go away within modern monetary architecture? Certainly not. As Christine Desan (2014) convincingly argues, modern money still thrives on elusive metaphors. It thrives, in part, on the naturalization of the political designs it is made of. And these designs involve most prominently, in the context of modern capitalism, the complicated problem of sharing a state monopoly of money creation with private investors. This precipitates an array of disputes about the kind of sovereignty these designs entail. Disputes also proliferate on the very meaning of money, though. It is at least curious – not to say crazy – that controversies abound today about the "nature" of money (the elementary fabric of social life, that is) among reputable economists, but also, more strikingly, among the experts in charge of central banking and monetary policy. The value of money is still a secret, it seems. Talk about the "alchemy of banking" can be heard in the medievalist symposium, but also, definitely, in the macroeconomics class.

The idea that wealth is wealth insofar as it is durably encapsulated within a durable vehicle – a fund, an estate, a trust – and managed accordingly also descends from medieval, theological doctrines of fortune and prosperity (Todeschini 2009). And it certainly forms a core tenet of financial imagination. This is the idea of a legitimate mechanism of entrustment, by virtue of which

the entitlement of the investor ought to be preserved throughout the process of the fructification
of value. An idea of fiduciary duty condensed in
the form of the legal trust, but also at work in any
common doctrine of corporate governance and
investor protection. Finance is certainly about
that. And paranoid finance explicitly draws from
a radicalized interpretation of this, as in the case
of OPPT varieties of the strawman theory and
their obsession with the legal trust form. The tri-
angle formed by settlor, trustee and beneficiary
acquires the contours of some sort of a financial
trinitarianism. But, as Giorgio Agamben (2009,
2011) suggests in his exploration of the theological genealogy of economic governance, this is just
the key to the formation of a notion of corporate
control. The coin of god has an economy, the
management of which requires a Trinity: that
is, a system of fiduciary duty tying a principal,
an agent and an asset together. The permanence
and circulation of value is the permanence and
circulation of will – the will of an original creator
(of value).

In fact – and here is where lies the kernel that
binds the delirious and the mainstream together –
the idea of value that forms financial imagination

is about revering the demiurgic power of a value creator, and about preserving that power from dissipation. And it is also about claiming, by all means possible, entitlement to that invisible substance and protection from rapine and dilapidation. Does the presence of a religious element there mean that this falls under the rubric of psychosis? Perhaps, at least potentially. This is a contentious claim, of course, as religious faith is commonly believed to be quite different from collective madness. And it certainly is. But there is an element of invisibility that needs to be borne in mind. An invisible substance calls easily for an invisible enemy. And making sense of things through that semiotic engine is inherently problematic.

One can certainly approach the business of making money with money without caring much about the jargon of value creation. But when that jargon controls the meaning of things, then the paranoid potential can thrive. Most centrally, this idea of value requires an idea of non-value: a menace, a demonic force of value destruction, a satanic double from which the treasure ought to be protected. The history of economic thought is loaded with such metaphors (Todeschini 2009,

2021). Indeed, QAnon narratives constitute a handy example of an obsession with the fundamental value of money being closely enmeshed within antisemitic myths (Rothschild 2021, 2023). More generally, if value is supposed to be "coming from us" out of some sort of a mixture between natural entitlement and spiritual force, then it means that it can be "taken away from us" – and is actually being taken away incessantly, almost by definition, as this menace is the semiotic condition that grants meaning to value. Paranoid finance just does the work of exacerbating a literal interpretation of the problematic keystone of economic value theory.

There is quite a difference between a "money for nothing" scheme, such as the one featured in the OPPT syndrome, and the principle of "making money with money" (also called "investment") that governs ordinary capitalistic rationality. But the two are in some conversation with each other. One would not create value out of nothing, a financier would claim. But so would a paranoid finance adept. The "seed money" (so to speak, with the words in use in the venture capital industry) that is needed for the happening of value creation is actual money, certainly.

But it also represents the intrinsic value of the venture capitalist, the visionary inspiration of the "business angel" (another industry metaphor) – an inner vibration that ought to be cultivated, treasured and remunerated accordingly. In a sense, paranoid finance would represent a radical democratization of the venture capital imagination: everyone as an angel investor, and everyone as the essential collateral asset too.

Stripped from their esoteric and conspiratorial elements, the varieties of paranoid finance examined here are in this respect comparable to the forms of popular emancipatory financial self-help analyzed by Daniel Fridman (2010, 2016). Counseling books, investment clubs, board games and online tutorials abound that promise financial freedom, often as part of some sort of a marketing scheme. These may often sound dubious to the expert ear, perhaps too enmeshed in a kind of populist, libertarian economic doctrine. It is all about freedom, yes, but freedom understood as freedom from a prevailing social order – a "rat race" – which is based on mandatory work, hierarchy, remuneration and taxation, and which can only be overcome through the crafty construction of personal financial rent.

A sort of radical state of personal sovereignty, then, based on the capacity to see everything in terms of assets – and quite attuned, it seems, to the salvific hopes of paranoid finance. But these forms of emancipatory financial self-help do also represent, albeit sometimes in a clumsy way, the mainstream drive toward the principal engine for the encoding of all things financial: so-called financial literacy (Lazarus 2020). And what is financial literacy about? It is about solving the most important problem society purportedly can encounter – i.e., a "financial crisis," understood as a breach in the rational valuation of the value of things – through the instillation, at all levels of said society, of the investor's style of thought.

And the same can be said of the kind of financial literacy that prevails in so-called high finance – that is, in the professional milieus of corporate and investment banking. By all ethnographic accounts, an investment bank is not a collection of free investors interacting seamlessly in a virtuous market. It instead very much looks like a "rat race" indeed, with its lot of mandatory work, hierarchy, remuneration and taxation. It is a bureaucratic organization, embedded in other bureaucratic organizations (that some call "the market"), in which the distribution of money is organized hierarchically, as well as the distribution of everything else (Godechot 2017; Ho 2009; Ortiz 2021). But the order of these hierarchies, as arbitrary as they may in fact seem from an external viewpoint, is justified by a body of knowledge – a semiotic engine, finance – at the center of which sits the idea that all should be as if all was allocated by free investors estimating freely the fundamental value of all, and freely interacting in a free market: financial imagination, as Horacio Ortiz (2014, 2021) calls this, showing how palpable and consequential the tensions and contradictions this imagination entails are inside an investment bank.

It can of course very well be the case that a financial analyst or an asset manager in a large investment bank carries on without indulging in value creation fantasies, and without spreading them. This is rather an exception, though, as the entire edifice is dependent on the semiotic machinery of financial valuation. Starting with the professional accreditation of that financial analyst and that asset manager, who are both required to memorize, exercise and apply proficiently the valuation methods that carry that semiotic machinery (Ortiz 2021). They also probably need to endure, in order just to aim at their top job in their top bank, the indoctrination process typically delivered in top business schools. The kind of top financial literacy found at work in these higher education organizations is remarkable for a number of reasons. It is far from being purely technical and contains an explicit spiritual dimension. Business is about rational financial valuation, but it is also about the courage to be a leader, take decisions and create value. Business schools also lay bare, however, the limits of that spiritual dimension.

Michel Anteby (2013) provides an ethnographic account of the crafting of the meaning of value (the value of things but also the value of oneself) at one of those top places, the Harvard Business School, which is of importance here. He shows the tensions in that process. On the one hand, there is a palpable obsession with value, one that has also been documented in historical studies of business education (Khurana 2007). Value creation is the most important thing, it is a mission, a vision, a guiding principle, a virtue: elevated and responsible at once. The Harvard Business School indeed stands as the paradigmatic case of a discourse in which the idea of "creating" value (as opposed to just "claiming" or, worse, "extracting" it) is pivotal. On the other hand, Anteby (2013) shows, it is a bit difficult to make sense of what this value exactly is about, if it needs to be about something more than just making money. Elevated, yes. But toward where? Responsible, yes. But for what? To a business school insider (as Anteby in part is), this sense of hollowness is something that can be quickly surpassed through rituals and routines. But to outsiders this really can look like a cult.

Cult-like value narratives are in fact there, displayed in the open, in many sites of the economic mainstream. One can immediately think of the prophetic tone adopted by reputable high-tech entrepreneurs ("visionaries" is the approved industry term), especially in sectors prone to futuristic ideation, such as biotechnology, computing and telecommunications. California – and the Silicon Valley, more specifically – may add to this tone a countercultural tinge, sometimes also psychedelic, as Fred Turner (2006) shows. Susi Geiger (2020) observes the demonic, eschatological elements at work in noted recent value ventures in healthcare technology and personal genomics. There is an obsession with the notion of the future, seen as something exhilarating and revolutionary, but also apocalyptic (this is always about a sort of an endgame), wrapped in the jargon of vision, disruption and also liberation – liberation of the body, or from the body, or of the soul, or from the soul, liberation of everything from everything else, in a kind of a transhumanist fashion (Taillandier 2021).

That value comes from the future (it is a return on investment) and that its creation requires some kind of courage and special foresight in the face of uncertainty are ideas that are well entrenched in the typical business school curriculum. And that the educated businessperson is also a thinker, a genius and an agent of civilization (or should aim at becoming so) is also part of the regular repertoire. But, here, these ideas acquire a superlative dimension. The value theory of the likes of Anne Wojcicki and Elizabeth Holmes, of Sergey Brin, Peter Thiel, Mark Zuckerberg, Elon Musk and Sam Altman, contains a blatant messianic element. It also reveals the contours of what Bruno Latour (2017) theorizes as some sort of an eschatological disinhibition, which is exacerbated in the apocalyptic extremes of the financial mind

(Samman and Sgambati 2023). Value creation is not just another name for capitalistic money-making. It is the foretelling gaze that allows for the overcoming of a doomed present – a present which happens in fact to be doomed, if at all, by the very engine of value creation.

That the formation and evolution of capitalism are conditioned by religion – secularized or not – is a truth that is perfectly well established in the sociological tradition. That capitalism is an essentially religious phenomenon is perhaps a more polemical statement (Löwy 2009). But the traction of such a statement is phenomenal when one observes the cultic, messianic structure and content of value narratives in dominant high-tech disruption milieus. If taken seriously, and literally, the civilizational musings about value creation, the meaning of life, and the future of society heard in the venture capital lounge sound just like paranoid finance. The Silicon Valley promises of extraordinary medical technologies considered by Geiger (2020) parallel indeed the redemptive undertones of the miracle cures (e.g., quantum medical sleeping pods that reverse aging, or "medbeds") dreamed of by QAnon influencers.

There is in paranoid finance the intuition that a law more fundamental than instituted human laws overrides them all. And that this fundamental law is the law of the creation and circulation of value. But this is, again, quite a recognizable ingredient of mainstream financial imagination too. There is certainly a deep sense of legal realism in the economic mainstream, with legions of lawyers telling legions of financiers how to comply with established institutions of law and order. This, however, combines with the incessant complaints about how too many laws and regulations stifle creative innovation, hamper entrepreneurial freedom and kill value creation. The naturalization of the law of value goes hand in hand with a critical exploitation of legal artifice.

The legalism inherent in paranoid finance echoes an insight that is well established in legal scholarship: namely, that wealth is an artifact of legal encoding, and that "investor protection" – the political shibboleth of financial capitalism – mostly requires astute, well-paid lawyers being good at the tricks of legal jargon and paperwork (Pistor 2019). The very fact that doctrines of corporate governance and investor protection become the engines of global power today, displacing standard regimes of state authority and shifting the rules of the world's economic game, is, to quite an extent, the consequence of the transformation of legal concepts (Robé 2020). Assessing specific jurisdictions in their capacity to comfort an investment gaze and recommending measures in order to improve their value friendliness become the accepted way to turn into policy a financial analysis of law (the so-called "Law and Finance" movement). The fact that state authority remains the ultimate source for the preservation of the key to financial value – private property, that is – combines with the fact that state authority is signaled as being a main obstacle of the liberation of value creation. And this paradox is not a bizarre contradiction that would be observable in paranoid finance only. This paradox is one constitutive tension of the political worldview contained in mainstream financial imagination.

Paranoid finance cultivates an obsession with the performative capacities of juristic artifice (Thomas 2021). On the one hand, pseudolaw thinking is obsessively preoccupied with the problem of the "legal fiction" (with the fictitious here understood as spurious, unreal and false) and develops an overt hostility toward any rule, institution or authority that would not emanate from a "natural" order (eternal, authentic and true). The naturalization of the laws of value creation coincides with a fundamentalist view of what creation means. On the other hand, though, pseudolegal litigation is emphatically consistent with a view for which the order of reality would be the performative outcome of legal or legalistic pronunciation: utterances, declarations, signatures, statements, rituals, syntaxes that establish a change in the configuration of reality, and which function almost as spells, curses or incantations. The fascination with Latin legal jargon, and, hence, with Roman law, is remarkable in relation to this paradox (see Appendix). Indeed, Yan Thomas (2021) situates in the operations of Roman law the origins of the juristic denaturalization of the world. But this performative power is also the instrument for naturalization – of the laws of value, for example.

Does this not just look like a clumsy version of the "Law and Finance" movement? Or of its holding paradigm, "Law and Economics"? The "and" is confusing in that expression, since there is a clear ascendancy in the hierarchy of these concepts: the doctrine that goes by that brand refers to an economic (or financial) analysis of law, certainly not to a legal analysis of finance. This means that the critical assessment of whatever happens in the realm of legal ordering is carried out through a lens that is superior in interpretive, explanatory and normative power: the lens of value creation and the protection thereof, hence the ultimate naturalization of the laws of value. The institutive capacity of legal artifice can then very well be decoded, critiqued and tinkered with, insofar as the actually superior legal order of the value creator is conveniently sanctified.

It is perhaps the case that paranoid finance and its approach to law reveals a characteristic feature of legal language at large: its critical instability and its potentials for self-disruption. A regime of signs, to use again the intuition put forward by Deleuze and Guattari (1983, 1987), that is at once overwhelmed by its own seriousness and spurred by its own indeterminacy. This is a development foreseen by Laurent de Sutter (2021), who submits the paradoxes of the performance of law to a reading in the terms of a philosophy of humor. The comicality and farcicality that critical observers tend to identify in pseudolegal litigation and argumentation often combine with appreciation of how well – or otherwise – the habits of instituted legal practice are mimicked there, which is an indirect way of telling how funny the latter in fact are. So it is perhaps the case that paranoid finance makes explicit, inadvertently, the inventive arbitrariness of the law of finance in general.

Take the obsession with contracts. Legal scholars examining sovereign citizen movements have rightly pointed out that, for pseudolegal influencers, absolutely everything is a contract, including one's relation to state authority. Engaging in exchange with an agent of law enforcement, for example, means entering a free, voluntary contractual relation that can be rightly repudiated. Critical legal scholars, however, are very well aware of the fact that mainstream financial imagination is also entirely obsessed with contracts. Everything, or almost everything, is a "nexus of contracts," abiding then, preferably, by the rule of some sort of contract law, when possible (Robé 2020). This applies to corporate governance and the so-called theory of the firm principally, but the potentials for the extension of the metaphor (for this is indeed an operative metaphor) are vast. And this obsession with contracts does not come from nowhere. It is firmly entrenched within the historical, liberal narrative of civil society. A narrative robustly naturalized in the concepts of freedom and coercion that form the backbone of liberal citizenship theory, as Margaret R. Somers (1995) shows, then further blended into financial imagination, in an era in which investment becomes the dominant metaphor for understanding one's place in society, as Gerald F. Davis (2009) tells.

And then comes the fantasy of sovereignty: the idea that provides paranoid finance with its legal highpoint, and which simultaneously presents mainstream financial imagination with its most intriguing political puzzle. The notion of sovereignty is indeed fragile, manifestly prone to affect and anxiety (Wall 2021). It requires a reference to some sort of a supreme authority – a sovereign, that is, a monarch of some sort, or even maybe some kind of divinity – in order to just make sense. There is a supernatural element at work in the formation of that concept, a theological genealogy, also perhaps a slightly pathological element of fantasy and simulacrum, and there is nothing polemical in signaling that (Derrida 2009, 2011). The trouble starts when the concept of sovereignty is meant to apply to the individual self – be it a "free investor" or a "living human soul" – or to a virtuous collective aggregate of individual selves – be it "the market" or "the one people" – within the context of the secular, democratic, modern state.

The trouble is not with the theological remnants that a secularization process may eventually have left untouched, then abandoning the modern age to some sort of illegitimacy (Blumenberg 1983). The trouble is rather with what this personal sovereignty ought to be defended from now: from the secular, democratic, modern state, precisely. Or, in other words, from the highly artificial web of bureaucratic, legal, political compromises that form the very possibility of anything akin to "sovereignty" in the present world. Participants in sovereign citizen movements, especially of the secessionist kind, are today sometimes very much obsessed with kings and queens, and with the sanctity of a people, a nation or a blood-line. And their sovereignty is explicitly posited against that of the modern state and its artifices. Asset managers and financial analysts might not share the same impetus. But they certainly, most officially, dream of secessionist jurisdictions (tax havens, pro-business states of exception, high-tech archipelagos) from which to fully enjoy the perspective of a sovereign free investor. And of doing this while looking at the so-called sovereign state as still a possible contractual party, an object of investment, to be valued accordingly – its debt being looked at with the disciplining eye of discounted cash flows (Blyth 2013; Lienau 2014).

The improvisational, cultic, conspiratorial, millennialist, esoteric, libertarian elements that one may find in paranoid finance do not represent a radical deviation from mainstream financial imagination. On the contrary, they represent a radicalization of financial imagination proper. An extremist, literal interpretation of the naturalization of the laws of value that mainstream financial capitalism thrives on. It is perhaps the case that finance is indeed in fact already paranoid finance, albeit in mufti or undercover. The semiotic engine of finance – the metaphor of value creation – contains the seed of a psychotic regime of signs (Deleuze and Guattari 1983, 1987). The dreams of financial reason produce in fact the monsters of paranoid finance.

The critique of finance

Paranoid finance is not short of paradoxes. It derives from mainstream financial imagination but is also posited, quite emphatically, as some sort of a critique of finance too. This does make sense, though. When the critique of finance is operated from the perspective of finance's innermost critical template – that of value creation – then things get out of hand. Like schizophrenia: a radical intensification of the critical eye, but an eye controlled by the terminology of what ought to be critiqued.

Paranoid finance borrows considerably – albeit in a somewhat altered manner – from mainstream critique of finance. The idea that states have been sneakily privatized to the benefit of a devious elite of globalist bankers with the purpose of extracting value from a deluded population is, in part, evocative of perfectly sensible analyses of neoliberal order and financial capitalism that have considerable currency in academic circles today. The idea of "surveillance capitalism" popularized by Shoshana Zuboff (2019) offers a case in point. True, it is a fact that there is a capitalistic obsession with behavioral data in the computing and telecommunication technology industry, an obsession from which stems the nightmare of a society entirely considered as an informational asset. To this is added the fact that capitalistic business is driven quite commonly by a monopolistic logic. There surely is something deeply worrying about this tide, which consists in turning everything into behavioral signals that ought to be managed with the purpose of value creation.

But how is this something about "human nature" (Zuboff 2019)? About some kind of a human primal truth whose "value" is being "scraped" in a kind of authoritarian fashion? Does effective critique require that one buys into the idea that one's behavioral whereabouts within an electronic platform correspond indeed to one's natural value? By that very same token, then, there is nothing wrong with this jargon of value creation. Only the fact that the original, legitimate proprietor of that inalienable value – oneself, one's own person, personhood and personality – has been abducted by some kind of an abstract "Big Other" (Zuboff 2019). The terminology is there, ready to be taken to the extreme. The terminology of some kind of a high-tech matrix in which candid individuals are reprogrammed – and their value sucked up – by an artificial, contrived power. The terminology of a critique that recognizes in the notion of value the ultimate compass for political emancipation. A value so fundamental and so veritable that it stands for nothing less than human nature. A value so precious and so great that its enemies can be nothing other than inhuman.

The enemies of value feature indeed as a key element in numerous critical narratives. Sometimes abstracted, fantasized as some sort of a structural force; other times, quite anthropomorphized, acquiring the contours of some kind of specific class of people or human type. In his sagacious and implacable critique of finance, for example, Wolfgang Streeck (2016) voices an intuition that is in fact quite commonly shared in critical academic circles and populist political milieus alike: namely, that the demise of the authority of the state in the face of financial institutions corresponds, at least in part, to a subordination of one kind of people (the nation – that is, the people of the nation-state) to another one (business elites, roughly considered, or what Streeck calls the "people of the market"). A denunciation of the limits of utopian universalism and of candid cosmopolitanism ensues, augmented with a vindication of pragmatic protectionism and measured nationalism. The vocabulary is there, though, available for a fuller exploitation of its political unconscious (Tooze 2017). In the radicalized terms of financial imagination, this is the people of true, fundamental value at war against the people of false, speculative value.

The notion of a globalist elite stands as perhaps a most recognizable token in this kind of mainstream critical discourse, but does also feature as a recurring leitmotiv in paranoid finance. This is a notion that circulates very well, for example, in the critical examination of the neoliberal tradition in political and economic thought. Quinn Slobodian (2018), for example, pertinently characterizes the conception spear-headed by Friedrich Hayek as a form of militant globalism, rather than as a mere variety of market fundamentalism. Neoliberalism is a doctrine that might remain opaque and difficult to decipher in full, as the overload of critical debate attests. But it ought to boil down to this: a dethronement of the nation, quite literally. A set of political precepts conducive to the constraint of nation-states (their people's sovereignty, that is) in favor of a so-called self-sustained "world economic order" – self-sustained, or, rather, sustained by its "guardians" (Slobodian 2018).

The notion of neoliberalism has a strong grip on the critical mind. Its critique fuels a critique of finance, or perhaps rather replaces it, stimu-lating an anti-globalist paradigm while easily accommodating a defense of a kind of capital-ism that would be national in essence, and thus good. Financial, but sovereign. That such images of a menacing world economic order can morph quite successfully into the conspiratorial ideation of a "New World Order" whose secretive, pow-erful guardians strive to implement a globalist agenda – and do that indeed in a not particu-larly liberal fashion – is a most substantial aspect of the intoxication paranoid finance represents. Against this: finance for the people, within the safe perimeter of its own sovereignty. But this is still finance, at its best. Finance defended by the critique of finance.

The notion of value that would actively feed that perspective is also insistently brewed within the critical mainstream. Calling value "speculative" or capital "fictitious" becomes a common feature within the vocabulary with which finance is dealt with in critical political economy, as exemplified by notable authors such as Cédric Durand (2017). It is easy to agree on the analytical traction that such wording may carry for a knowledgeable economist. But it is also quite evidently full of philosophical mess, fostering as it does a representation of one kind of money that would be real and another one that would not, one kind of value that would be true and another one that would not. Value that is true and value that is not: exactly the semiotic engine that one should be expected to be critical with when dealing with the power of finance. The engine remains untouched. Worst, it is actively boosted. The true value of judicious, veritable financial investment, against the false value of whimsical, unfair market speculation. This being eventually augmented, if needed, with the anthropological type of choice: the enrooted national people against the rootless globalist league.

Should (or can) economists emancipate themselves from the very notion that forms the kernel of both their discipline and financial imagination? This is certainly quite demanding. It will require a state of philosophical awareness that might indeed damage the very cultural foundations of the entire edifice of standard economic thought. It is nonetheless necessary to pay attention to the damage that those cultural foundations do already bear: their contradictions, the trouble inherent in them, their contiguity to political delirium.

Philosophical critique is itself not immune to the semiotic engine of finance. A sophisticated promotion of the rhetoric of value creation can be found even in critical work that is, curiously enough, explicitly grounded in a tradition of poststructuralist, deconstructionist, radical philosophy. This is, for example, the case of the call for a "revaluation of value" developed by Brian Massumi (2018), an author who is known for his contribution to the dissemination of the work of

Deleuze and Guattari. The idea that value remains constrained by oppressive powers, that it should be reclaimed and unlocked, and its potentials joyfully unleashed, combines there with an explicit vindication of the financial market (a community for deciding freely what is valuable and how to boost that value) as a source of inspiration for an alternative to dominant interpretations of money. The fact that cryptocurrencies quite naturally feature there, in that call, as a vehicle for creative emancipation confirms the potentiality of a deleterious trajectory toward paranoid finance.

It is, to be sure, possible to recognize in these and comparable stances a number of stereotypes that are at work in conspiratorial financial fantasy. Does this mean that the critique of finance, formulated in those terms, inevitably leads to the delusional space of paranoid finance? Or does this rather mean that paranoid finance inevitably distorts the demanding language of incisive critical knowledge? A bit of both. The trouble is not with critique's critical impetus, but rather with a premise. Mainstream critique of the financial order shares with paranoid finance the very semiotic engine of finance. Indeed, they both rely on a radicalization of the notion of value, a notion cemented in the tradition of political economy and liberal philosophy, and further refined within the medium of financial imagination.

The critique of finance can lead to imaginative attempts to circumvent the inherited codes of financial imagination, though. This is, for instance, the case with proposals stemming from heterodox approaches to debt and currency that unravel, at least in part, dominant narratives of money creation, and that are generally grounded in a legal comprehension of finance, and in a genuinely democratic preoccupation (e.g., Grey 2021; Hockett 2020; Omarova 2021). These definitely side with a constructivist approach to the institutions of monetary culture, and with a careful understanding of the tangles and potentials of minting, for example, in a digital environment. Their possible exposure to narratives of magical currency, of free infinite money, and of sovereign citizens naturally entitled to their own natural value is, alas, not negligible. The traps of paranoid finance – and, for that matter, of a constructivist worldview for which value, whatever that is supposed to mean, would "come from us" – are numerous and subtle.

Another critique of finance is yet possible. One that does not draw from the critical energy that finance itself charges the notion of value with. One that does not abide by the categories of political economy, not even of critical political economy. One that rather opts for a critique of political economy, a critique that would dissect the anachronism of the very notion of value developed there – as Moishe Postone (2017) has it. It is this critical stance – a critique of value as a political fetish – that would allow overcoming the impasses represented by paranoid finance, in both its mild forms and its most atrocious varieties (Postone 1980). A critique of finance that would start, precisely, with a critique of the opposition between a natural sphere of fundamental value, on the one side, and, on the other, a contrived order of speculative value from which the precious source of value creation ought to be protected.

Sensitivity toward the spectral quality of the categories of financial value needs to be developed, then – of "fundamental" and "speculative" value alike, as Joseph Vogl (2014) suggests in part, signaling in addition the insidious modes of anxiety and animosity this semiotic engine involves

(Vogl 2022). It is certainly about breaking a spell, as Philippe Pignarre and Isabelle Stengers (2011) put it. But the spell to be broken is the spell of value. And a spell cannot be broken with the very instrument of the incantation. The enemy is not the enemy of value. The enemy is value itself.

This kind of critique may certainly sound ugly to the financial ear, be it critical or not, paranoid or not. Yes, it may sound like a call for the destruction of value. Destruction of the concept of value, at least – of its interpretive power and its political traction. Destruction of its theological unconscious and of its moral glow, too. From the perspective of the discourse of paranoid finance, this is exactly about siding with the enemies of value. Befriending them, becoming a guardian of their order. Quite intimidating, for sure. But what does critique mean, if not emancipation from the ascendancy of an inherited concept?

Critique can be many things. It can be – and regularly is – about telling as wisely as possible the good from the bad, the true from the false, the fair from the unfair, the worthwhile from the worthless. And, then, all that critique means depends quite evidently on the point of view, because what can be good here can also be bad there or elsewhere. But critique can be something else. It can be about pressuring the conditions in which things do make sense. About interrogating the threshold above which the meaning of something dissolves or collapses. This is philosophical critique, then, carried out for the sake of establishing how does a concept work, or does not. And also for the sake of spotting the troubles this meaning may prompt. And this should work for finance. It should work for the semiotic engine it consists of, and for the cultural syndrome it forms.

Is this sort of philosophical critique not, in a sense, akin to psychoanalytical critique? Maybe it is. It is definitely about paying attention to the terms in which the trouble is expressed, neither fully endorsing nor fully debunking those terms – rather, capturing the echoes they carry. And seeing where these echoes can come to exhaustion. This is what it means, in a way, to examine what the echoes of the liberal subject become when they are lost in paranoia (Beckman 2022; Melley 2000). This point of exhaustion is where the limits of meaning – the limits of financial imagination, here – become explicit. And where critique can eventually be exerted from outside these limits. With other terms. At least with terms other than those imposed by the trouble itself – here, value.

Paranoia disappears when the paranoiac starts laughing about it, as François Roustang (1987) puts it. That is why paranoia is so serious, so totalizing. So totalitarian. Paranoia is about preventing oneself from losing one's own limits, preventing that at all costs, even if this demands provoking a state of persecution, in order to reaffirm one's own contours, and incessantly reestablishing the certainty of enmity. In other words, paranoia puts oneself in the position of guarantor of truth. Making fun of that – of truth and its guardians – is a dangerous business. It creates a space for equivoque and drift. It can even be taken as some sort of a solidarity in madness, as if the cure would consist in some kind of a replication of psychosis. But it works as a condition for the alleviation of the symptoms. And then, perhaps, also as a condition for critique: a critique that may succeed where paranoia has failed.

Conclusion

So finance is paranoid finance. And the critique of finance is paranoid finance too. And this stays so, unless something is done about the core engine of financial meaning, which contains the paranoid potential. For this engine is value. Value and value creation. It rules by virtue of the controlling metaphor of an invisible substance that irrigates the body economic, whose source ought to be praised and secured, and its mysterious fundament defended. A metaphor that requires, in order to make sense, a menace of depredation, and a promise of value panic. True value pitted against false value, offered in many guises, but always reminiscent of a spiritual element: a specter, a fetish, a fantasy, a phantasm, a hallucination, a hollow foundation. Fundamental value pitted against speculative value, unless the conditions are met for speculation to become a sheer recognition of the fundamental truth of a return on investment that comes from the future and that ought to be gauged courageously in the midst of uncertainty. Value creation, then.

But this is the semiotic engine of finance. The rhetorical apparatus from which finance gets its power: the power to control the meaning of things. And the power to control the critique of finance too, when it ends up buying into the terminology of value. This is a terminology full of toxic metaphors that, if taken too seriously, too literally, too fervently, open a door to political disorientation and existential disarray. Paranoid finance becomes then, at one and the same time, the ultimate recipe for critical dissent and the radical vehicle for ideological conformity.

What should be done, then? The response to this escapes the usual binaries that juxtapose reason against insanity or order against disorder. It is rather about seeing in insanity a symptom of reason, and in disorder a consequence of order – of financial reason and financial order. A critical assessment of contemporary conspiratorial, millennialist discourse on money, finance, wealth and value is undoubtedly needed. Syndromes such as the ones examined here certainly represent a series of worrying dangers, as they contain strong elements of distress, enmity, delusion, faith and violence. But they also contain strong elements of standard financial imagination. They nurture an ideal of true value creation that ought to be unbound, of moral entitlement to a fund that needs to be protected from expropriation, of financial sovereignty as the ultimate political goal, and of emancipation through the smart exploitation of cracks in the juristic edifice of the modern state. The dream of paranoid finance is in fact that of a world populated with free, sovereign investors who are at once producers of currency, beneficiaries of value, and proprietors of themselves: "value asset centers" that interact through voluntary contracts and form a virtuous web of eternal, seamless valorization. But this is the dream of finance. And this dream carries its inevitable defensive counterpart: that of a treasure that needs to be protected from the sacrilegious hordes of the false faith.

Paranoid finance thus operates as an immanent critique of finance, a critique that stems from an intensification of the rationality of finance itself. Its dangers, then, reflect the dangers of finance. Value – the notion of value that forms the crux of financial imagination – stands as its prodromal element. This is surely a contentious claim. It implies that a critique of financial imagination, and of the ideal of value that is entrenched within it, needs to precede a viable critique of paranoid finance. This requires putting the notion of value aside altogether, or, at least, refraining from using it as a compass for a critique of financial reality. This requires also reconsidering judgment of the claims found in paranoid finance. In many ways these claims are decidedly dubious, but so are concepts and claims that undergird conventional finance. The discourse of paranoid finance deserves attention, then. It operates, in part, as a radically literal interpretation of the concepts of financial rationality, thus making their unsettling potential explicit.

Paranoid finance offers an opportunity to revisit the intuition that Deleuze and Guattari (1983, 1987) put together in their *Capitalism and Schizophrenia*: the intuition of an inherent trouble in the semiotic engine of capitalistic value. This engine certainly demands critique. But it also asks that a critical approach take things with a pinch of salt. For critique cannot merely be about repressing the delirious potential contained in financial imagination. It cannot be just about denouncing the phantasm, and then about silencing it. It should be, rather, about learning from it: learning from its tortuous pursuit of the restoration of meaning. For the phantasm fulfills a function, and that function is none other than realization (Deleuze 1990).

Appendix: transcript of tutorial

What follows is the condensed transcript of one OPPT ("One People's Public Trust") meeting, edited from personal field notes. The account is based on the examination of the recording of a 4-hour-long online study group conference, held in May 2021 using video-conferencing software and uploaded by the conference host to a public online video platform. The conference consisted of an introduction to OPPT delivered by one practitioner for a group of about 50 participants. The meeting was the first of a series that raised the profile of this particular OPPT community all over the world, prompting increasing participation (this file received about 200,000 views a year since being posted, according to the indications provided by the video platform). The anonymity of host and participants is preserved here. This material has been collected as part of a wider empirical investigation. The study is based on the qualitative analysis of a collection of more than 100 audiovisual files gathered from a popular public online video platform, from September 2021 to September 2023. The collection principally includes OPPT tutorials and discussions posted by practitioners, in a number of languages (English, Spanish, French, Italian). The selection of the materials follows a snowball approach, with relevant materials identified through OPPT keywords, references to particular practitioners within a community, links to and citations of other materials, and indications of popularity (such as views or comments).

About 50 people attend this online meeting. Most seem to be quite new to OPPT, while some have already initiated some practical work. The host declares at the outset that this is an ongoing investigation. The host is still learning about all this, connecting to other communities, studying the "documents" OPPT wisdom is made of, and trying out some action. It is the spring of 2021. The significance of the context of the global COVID-19 epidemic is palpable: policies such as the requirement of vaccine passports, restrictions on movement, and mandatory face masks are considered by most participants as authoritarian measures, and OPPT is in part an instrument to establish personal sovereignty that will allow the achievement of liberation from the system. The "system" is portrayed throughout the meeting in terms of enmity – there is a "them," and there is an "us" that refers to a community (a "vibration") which is expanding through the world. The narrative delivered by the host is at times quite assertive and sophisticated, at other times hesitant and somewhat contradictory. The host uses a slideshow in order to convey the main ideas (about 70 slides in total). The meeting lasts 4 hours. This is the first of a series of meetings in which ideas will be refined, better knowledge will be constructed, and particular tactics and problems will be addressed. In addition to the online meeting and the public dissemination of its recording, this community interacts through instant messaging and file-sharing platforms. The host has also published a website where documents and tutorials are posted. There is excitement among the participants. Important and difficult knowledge is about to be clarified, at least in part.

The following abridged notes are paraphrasing what was said, with the purpose of documenting the meandering narratives that feed this particular variety of paranoid finance.

Transcript of notes, edited

It is all about personal sovereignty, freedom from slavery. We live in a state of slavery, but this slavery is hardly visible. We are born into bondage and remain blind to it. This is really like the famous line from the movie *The Matrix*: the truth is that we are born into a prison that we cannot see, a prison for our mind.

It is all about value, too. The state of bondage we live in amounts to the alienation of our value. This is theft. Where does value come from? It comes from us. We are the value. Value stems from one's living essence. But value has been taken away from us and monetized in a complicated manner. We are the source of the value represented by money flows, but this generative link has been concealed from us so that we perceive ourselves as being indebted to the institutions that manage these money flows. For example, when we go to a bank to get a loan, the money we get comes from a fund that is, in fact, already ours. So we should not pay for it.

It all starts with the birth certificate; this is the key device in the machinery of bondage. At birth, our

parents comply with the basic requirement of registering our existence with a dedicated government
office. But there, without them being aware, our
original name is transformed into something else:
that of a "person," which is a legal fiction. This
second name is always capitalized. Capitalization
is the mark of the legal fiction. In administrative paperwork, our name is capitalized because
this denotes a form of "decapitation," as the Latin
concept of *capitis deminutio* attests: a juristic concept that refers to the loss of legal capacity and
the deprivation of liberty. But this is not us; this
is only our "strawman," from which we should
detach.

This leads again to value – and money. This legal
fiction aims indeed at granting every one of us
corporate personhood so that one can be treated as
a corporation, that is, treated as if one were dead.
The meaning of "corporation" relates indeed to
"corpse." A "person" has "no body," is "nobody."
One obvious purpose of this is to claim money from
us, in the form of taxes or fines. But a more sophisticated scheme consists in using us (or, rather, our
fictional corporate personhood, our "strawman")
as collateral for the state's money. Indeed, one

single birth certificate is secretly valued within this scheme in millions of dollars.

The crucial vehicle for this slavery scheme is a "trust": a forced trust in which the parent representing the newborn is, unknowingly, the settlor, and the state is both the trustee and the beneficiary. The entrusted property (the "bond") is none other than us, our value and the right to claim it. After a period of seven years, the trustee observes that the entrusted property is not reclaimed. Then the newborn is declared "lost at sea," which opens the way to the use of admiralty law. The state hence takes possession of the bond. The birth certificate can thus work as collateral, or guarantee, for the state to access credit in the international financial system. All trust files, including all birth certificates, are kept on record in Washington, DC.

All this is possible because today all states are, in fact, private corporations. All but five states (Russia, China, Iran, Libya and North Korea) are registered as such with the Securities and Exchange Commission (SEC), a US federal agency created in 1933 for the purpose of serving as a registry for corporations. This is easily verifiable through a search in the public database of SEC filings. For example, the Republic of Italy is registered as a corporation (headquartered in Washington, DC). Indeed, in 1933, 194 nations were covertly registered as corporations with the SEC, as part of an international plan to construct a new global financial order.

Therefore, what we usually refer to as countries, or nations, or sovereign states, are in fact private corporations, ruled by principles of US private law. They abide by the Uniform Commercial Code (UCC), the body of norms that govern the regulation of commercial transactions within and across US states. The SEC stands as a court for the settlement of issues between corporations, and the UCC stands as the SEC's legislative code, which applies to all countries since they were turned into private corporations. States registered as private corporations thus act as private corporations, which means that they are interested in getting money for their owners, not in the public good.

It is important at this point to understand the true hierarchies of legal authority. The first order of law, the one that ultimately prevails, is natural law. This refers to universal principles, which are obvious, observable in the rules of the natural world and of human nature, and which stand as legal principles even if they are not enacted in the form of positive law or normative procedure. The institution of the people's tribunal is the highest possible court, since it is the highest approximation to natural law, being as it is based on the rule of natural humanity. The rest of the legal orders are inferior in authority.

Maritime law, also known as admiralty law, is a relevant legal order here. Maritime law has been in use since the times of the Sumerian and Babylonian empires and stands typically as the primary source for commercial law and the law of corporations. It applies to banks, money, cash flows, things that are "liquid" and "fluid," like the sea.

Canon law is the fundamental source for today's standing legal order. It is derived from Roman law, the body of legal doctrine that cemented the bases of the doctrine of slavery. The Roman notion of *capitis deminutio*, recognizable in today's administrative language, governs the loss of freedom. The notion of *pater familias* also refers to slavery, with emancipation (*emancipatio*) consisting in a process of liberation, albeit limited, from that power (*potestas*) through the constitution of oneself as *sui iuris* – that is, a legally competent agent. Today, the state behaves quite obviously as a *pater familias* toward us, granting us some legal capacity, but in a limited way. We can sign contracts, but we lack the legal authority needed to question and transform the terms of a contract (e.g., one can purchase a house, but must go through a properly appointed notary in order to set the terms).

The law is in fact a concealed art, an art of the occult, the sophistication of which is exemplified by the House of Medici and its skillful control of commerce (the corporations, or guilds, that organized and operated the arts and trades) in the Republic of Florence in early Renaissance Italy. The art of the Medicis was one of infiltration and corruption, which included a dexterous manipulation of legal concepts. Most of our legal concepts are corrupted.

Most of our words, in fact, are corrupted, and this does not apply only to legal concepts. This is part of the problem. A general effort to reconstruct our language is needed. For example, we call ourselves persons, but "person" means "mask," which is the opposite of what we want to mean when we talk about ourselves as recognizable, living human beings. Take the English word "world": it is connected to the words "sword" and "word," which therefore convey, occulted, the idea that "the word is a sword for the world." And take the concept of "attorney," which is derived from Latin *ad* (to) and *tornus* (turn) – that is, to turn away from one's rights. The attorney is literally there to demonstrate that we have surrendered our rights. Same for "barrister" – *baro* (simpleton, stupid) and *sto* (standing firm) – therefore, representing an incompetent. According to today's legal standards, we need a lawyer in order to defend our rights. But getting a lawyer actually means declaring that we are not capable of defending ourselves, and that therefore we do not have rights. This is the work of the art of legal fiction – to conceal our true value and our true power.

These fictions, encapsulated in the device of the birth certificate, do not correspond to our true essence. These are artifacts, constructions, interfaces through which the state interacts with legal subjects, asking that we identify with these. When we "register" the birth certificate, we are unknowingly signing a contract by which we transfer (*registrum*, i.e., to carry, to transfer) the newborn to the state. That is why the state can take away our children – because it is the owner. But this is but a contract, and contracts can be repudiated, broken or terminated.

So our task is to recover our value, the true value that we have as living humans (*homo vivo*). No living human is above another living human, except in the case of voluntary acceptance. No law written by a human can be imposed on another human. All humans can reject, modify or rewrite a human law. This means that, in order for a living human being to be subjected to the laws and regulations of a fellow human being, plain, written consent is required. This is an essential principle of natural law.

The genuine holder of true rights is always the soul. This means the divine, embodied essence of the "I am." This is usually conflated with the notion of the person. But these are completely different notions, and that conflation is a trick meant to conceal the truth. This is key for understanding the paperwork involved in current declarations of sovereignty. Such paperwork is the expression of a truth that requires previous, deep understanding. It requires an examination of how religions appropriate basic truths in order to conceal them.

Christianity is presented to the masses as a godly religion. But the Catholic Church operates a form of pagan satanic cult. They are worshipers of Saturn, the "black star," and their cult is recognizable through the geometric figures that appear in their symbols and emblems. The hexagon features in many symbols, as does the cube: both are marks of the cult of Saturn, together with the representation of the rings of Saturn. One can easily recognize these shapes also in Judaism (e.g., the black cube in the phylacteries and the hexagon inside the hexagram of the Star of David) and Islam (e.g., the Kaaba in Mecca, which contains a meteorite around which worshipers revolve like the rings of Saturn). The "meditation room" at the headquarters of the United Nations also contains a black cube. And many brand logos feature a reference to the rings of Saturn. And the color black is present in all religious and legal attire, also in police uniforms. All rituals, all false.

Further pagan symbols firmly and visibly stand in the centers of global power, such as the obelisk, to be found in the City of London, the Vatican City, and Washington, DC: all three are independent jurisdictions that control the world (financially, religiously and militarily, respectively). Washington, DC, is the center of military power and also the jurisdiction in which our birth certificates are stored.

The "trust" is part of all this. Pope Boniface VIII was the architect of a crucial device that embodied the idea of the trust: the papal bull of 1302 (*Unam sanctam*). The trust operated as follows: the settlor is god, the pope is both the trustee and the beneficiary, and the fund is the entire world and its inhabitants. The Vatican owns the world. The bull stood as a pristine vehicle for papal domination – and for the enslavement of the creation. The trust is based on Noah's ark, which explains the relevance of admiralty law (all "lost at sea"). Pope Boniface VIII used his own blood for ink, on vellum made from the skin of a sacrificed baby: black magic indeed. We are still under the spell of that terrible human sacrifice.

A further crucial element in the construction of the trust mechanism is the *Cestui que vie* Act of 1666 of the Parliament of England, a presumption of death statute that was used in order to declare every person over the age of seven dead and "lost at sea." Every living human being is thus considered legally incompetent and placed in a state of *interdictum* and effectively ruled, through the artifact of juristic person, by admiralty law. In short, living human beings are legally turned into commodities. The state becomes the trustee of all titles, of all the value of human beings, unless a living human being comes back from being "lost at sea" and reclaims that title.

In 2012, all this system was demolished or at least fatally undermined by a most virtuous initiative, carried out by a group of people that had revealed its mechanisms. It was the establishment of a trust, the One People's Public Trust, or OPPT 1776, which reinstated the original Constitution of the United States of America, which had been corrupted, and restored the Thirteenth Amendment, which abolishes slavery and involuntary servitude. It aimed at bringing back the spirit of the original trust of 1776 (the year of the Declaration of

Independence), of which the people of the United States stood as beneficiaries. The original trust had been supplanted in 1871 by a new trust set up by the Rockefeller family, with the "US Corporation" as the trustee and with the Rockefeller heirs, then also, through a series of complicated mechanisms, the Rothschild heirs and George Soros, as the beneficiaries. The 2012 new trust was conveniently and lawfully filed under the UCC. It was designed as follows: the settlor is the creator, and the beneficiary is the eternal essence. And the trustees – Heather Ann Tucci-Jarraf, Caleb Paul Skinner and Hollis Randall Hillner – are the artisans of this liberating scheme.

OPPT 1776 automatically blocked the effectiveness of the jurisdiction of the SEC and also forced the foreclosure of all states registered as corporations, thus canceling, *de iure* (by law), their operation. In short, the authority of states has been suspended ever since. The process consisted in the careful filing of up to 50 or more different documents according to the UCC procedure (e.g., registering a series of UCC financing statements), lawfully considering that an absence of rebuttal means acceptance and therefore enactment of these documents as legitimate law. If we all follow the process carefully, the whole system will collapse.

OPPT 1776 flows from the legal oath of the three trustees, who act in the name of the eternal essence in order to restore universal natural law and therefore to return the value of the "one people" to its beneficiaries, which are all free, living human beings on earth. Nothing, no law, stands legally above this trust, which is today an indisputable law.

This process started in the United States, but then spread internationally. The US community suffered a crisis, due to adverse circumstances that led to the incarceration of Heather Ann Tucci-Jarraf. But now it is flourishing again all over the world: it is strong in Italy, for example. A process of circulation of energy, of karma, guides the spread of this realization. A number of people are achieving the revocation of their tax payments, the recovery of ownership over their vehicles, and the issuing of universal travel licenses. There is one person in Italy who actually succeeded in reclaiming 100 million dollars. There exist channels in online social networks in which all this is shared and developed.

Back in the times of the proclamation of OPPT, Heather discovered how to access our birth certificate bonds and published a tutorial on how to recover them and redeem their value. But, due to the ill behavior of one participant who incurred excessive expenditures, Heather was accused of fraud and arrested in 2017, precisely at a time when she was in contact with President Donald Trump to explain the OPPT to him. This exchange with Heather probably inspired Trump's approach to the crisis of US sovereignty.

But the most important fact is that OPPT 1776 effectively prevented governments all over the world from accessing the fund constituted by our birth certificates and using it as collateral in the financial markets. That is precisely why international organizations such as the United Nations are now defending the need for what they call a "new social contract": it is very clear that they mean a new trust scheme that would allow them to recover access to our value.

Heather declared the "we is": the apparent grammar error is purposeful; it conveys the logic of the new paradigm, "we" is "I am." This means that

the OPPT 1776 UCC documents do not constitute only a material fact. They have a spiritual
dimension. They are a vehicle for the energetic
deprogramming of an inverted matrix. The inten-
tion is to awaken our natural, eternal essence, to
revive the spark of creation that is in all of us. We
need to establish a new connection, with life and
among ourselves. And this movement is unstop-
pable. We are about to overturn the old mental
paradigm, which is grounded in ancient archetypes
of fear and guilt, ancient programs of holographic
induction.

There are other initiatives and movements that
compare to OPPT. But there are plenty of traps.
NESARA/GESARA is a trap, obviously. It is
entirely based on a return to the gold standard. But
this is business as usual: a currency standard. And
it is based on the flawed idea that value comes from
gold. Since gold is alchemically the materialization
of light, these people, who like to play with magic,
developed a fixation with gold. They also wor-
ship the idea of scarcity and lack. Heather's is an
entirely different idea. We are the universal crea-
tors of value. We are not ruled by the value of gold.
Value comes from us: we are the value standard.

Heather established the I-UV Exchange, or Universal Value Exchange, a system that operates accounts of "we is." Heather seized all the banks in the world except the Bank of International Settlements (BIS) in Basel, which is the bank that manages all the banks. She did that in order to prevent the global economic system from collapsing. We want to create a transition, not to destroy everything. She declared, as a penalty ("remedy") for the discovered fraud, the sums of 5 billion dollars in gold for every living human's soul and 5 billion in silver for the body. She established that every one of us could access that value at any moment. That is why the BIS needed to be kept standing, in order for us to access that value. One will be able to request one's account from the BIS. It just needs to be done properly. It is a cash flow account that we can access from any bank. The funds there are unlimited. We produce money as an act of will. We can pay for everything we want with it.

It is all about handling carefully the filing of the documents laid out initially by the trustees of OPPT 1776. There are several such documents. One important one is known as "Military Order." It consists of two parts. The first one, "Declaration and Order," asserts that the state has committed an act of treason. The document is meant to be sent or shown to military authorities, ordering them to desist from using force against living human beings and to arrest all state agents involved in the enforcement of the slavery system. The second part is a UCC "Financing Statement Amendment" by which the trustees extend the collateral of the trust to all creation. Another essential document is the "I Am Declaration," by virtue of which we demonstrate that we are alive (not "lost at sea"), and we regain full jurisdiction over our legal fictions. It is all a perfect edifice of documents that fit into each other. Proof that Heather was really inspired by the ultimate source.

Another essential document is the "Declaration of Original Depository and Deposit of I Am" (DODD), which establishes the signatory as a living, conscious, free human being that stands, at one and the same time, as the original depository and the source of value, the value of eternal essence. The document confirms that this value cannot be estimated – it is unlimited. This is important because from this follows that we can access our value deposit unlimitedly. Because we are, simultaneously, the source of value and the depository of the soul. Additional documents ("Declaration of Original Conversion" and "Declaration of Receipt") further secure the process, unwinding the matrix and unlocking the 10 billion dollars in gold and silver that we lawfully own, whose value is unceasingly revalued, finally considered as a deposit of the eternal essence.

Other documents are meant to safeguard the process, protecting it from harmful enemies. The "Courtesy Notice" aims at notifying individuals we need to interact with, and who are meant to represent corporate actors (e.g., bank branch employees, civil servants, police officers, tax officers), that their corporate power is null due to the foreclosure of all corporations, and that they act only as individuals with full liability for their actions. They believe they are enforcing rules, but in fact they are only proposing contracts. Contracts that we duly reject, "in good honor and without prejudice" (that is, reserving our right not to be compelled to perform under any contract that we did not enter voluntarily). The recipient has to respond before a deadline (28 days). The absence of response means acceptance. When the notice contains a formal accusation, its acceptance means that a penalty, or "remedy," can follow – for example, the issuing of an invoice for compensation. The notice ought to be properly signed, even with one's own blood, to provide it with more energy.

Not everyone understands all this. We often meet people who do not get it and see us as a threat. Like in *The Matrix*. The system is certainly against us, but also friends, acquaintances, neighbors and relatives can be against us when we say "I am." Rather than being confrontational, we should be generous. What we ought to do is create a vibration, an energy, and ignore the ones that cannot or do not want to feel it. They will disappear anyway.

References

Agamben, G. (2009), *What is an Apparatus? And Other Essays*, Stanford University Press.

Agamben, G. (2011), *The Kingdom and the Glory: For a Theological Genealogy of Economy and Government*, Stanford University Press.

Agnew, J.-C. (1986), *Worlds Apart: The Market and the Theater in Anglo-American Thought, 1550–1750*, Cambridge University Press.

Alliez, É. (1996), *Capital Times: Tales from the Conquest of Time*, University of Minnesota Press.

Anteby, M. (2013), *Manufacturing Morals: The Values of Silence in Business School Education*, University of Chicago Press.

Barkun, M. (2003), *A Culture of Conspiracy:*

Apocalyptic Visions in Contemporary America, University of California Press.

Barman, E. (2016), *Caring Capitalism: The Meaning and Measure of Social Value*, Cambridge University Press.

Barrows, S. (2021), "Sovereigns, freemen, and desperate souls: towards a rigorous understanding of pseudolitigation tactics in United States courts," *Boston College Law Review*, 62(3), 905–40.

Beckman, F. (2022), *The Paranoid Chronotope: Power, Truth, Identity*, Stanford University Press.

Bloom, M., and S. Moskalenko (2021), *Pastels and Pedophiles: Inside the Mind of QAnon*, Stanford University Press.

Blumenberg, H. (1983), *The Legitimacy of the Modern Age*, MIT Press.

Blumenberg, H. (2010), *Paradigms for a Metaphorology*, Cornell University Press.

Blyth, M. (2013), *Austerity: The History of a Dangerous Idea*, Oxford University Press.

Boltanski, L., and A. Esquerre (2020), *Enrichment: A Critique of Commodities*, Polity.

Burwell, J. (2013), "Figuring matter: quantum physics as a New Age rhetoric," *Science as Culture*, 22(3), 344–66.

Crockford, S. (2021), *Ripples of the Universe: Spir-*

ituality in Sedona, Arizona, University of Chicago Press.

Crockford, S. (2022), "How to manifest abundance: money and the rematerialization of exchange in Sedona, Arizona, USA," *Journal of the Royal Anthropological Institute*, 28(3), 920–37.

Davis, G. F. (2009), *Managed by the Markets: How Finance Reshaped America*, Oxford University Press.

Deleuze, G. (1990), *The Logic of Sense*, Columbia University Press.

Deleuze, G., and F. Guattari (1983), *Anti-Oedipus: Capitalism and Schizophrenia*, University of Minnesota Press.

Deleuze, G., and F. Guattari (1987), *A Thousand Plateaus: Capitalism and Schizophrenia*, University of Minnesota Press.

Derrida, J. (2009), *The Beast and the Sovereign*, Volume I, University of Chicago Press.

Derrida, J. (2011), *The Beast and the Sovereign*, Volume II, University of Chicago Press.

Desan, C. (2014), *Making Money: Coin, Currency, and the Coming of Capitalism*, Oxford University Press.

Deville, J. (2015), *Lived Economies of Default: Consumer Credit, Debt Collection and the Capture of Affect*, Routledge.

Dodd, N. (2014), *The Social Life of Money*, Princeton University Press.

Doganova, L. (2024), *Discounting the Future: The Ascendancy of a Political Technology*, Zone Books.

Durand, C. (2017), *Fictitious Capital: How Finance Is Appropriating Our Future*, Verso.

Eco, U. (1983), "The scandal of metaphor: metaphorology and semiotics," *Poetics Today*, 4(2), 217–57.

Faux, Z. (2023), *Number Go Up: Inside Crypto's Wild Rise and Staggering Fall*, Currency.

Fenster, M. (2008), *Conspiracy Theories: Secrecy and Power in American Culture*, University of Minnesota Press.

Foucault, M. (1970), *The Order of Things: An Archaeology of the Human Sciences*, Pantheon Books.

Fridman, D. (2010), "From rats to riches: game playing and the production of the capitalist self," *Qualitative Sociology*, 33(4), 423–46.

Fridman, D. (2016), *Freedom from Work: Embracing Financial Self-Help in the United States and Argentina*, Stanford University Press.

Geiger, S. (2020), "Silicon Valley, disruption, and the end of uncertainty," *Journal of Cultural Economy*, 13(2), 169–84.

Gerard, D. (2017), *Attack of the Fifty Foot Blockchain:*

Bitcoin, Blockchain, Ethereum and Smart Contracts, CreateSpace.

Godechot, O. (2017), *Wages, Bonuses and Appropriation of Profit in the Financial Industry: The Working Rich*, Routledge.

Goldman, M. (2022), "From Bitcoin to DeFi (in 12 short years)," *Bloomberg*, 19 January 2022: www.bloomberg.com/news/videos/2022-01-19/from-bitcoin-to-defi-in-12-short-years-video.

Golumbia, D. (2016), *The Politics of Bitcoin: Software as Right-Wing Extremism*, University of Minnesota Press.

Grey, R. (2021), "Administering money: coinage, debt crises, and the future of fiscal policy," *Kentucky Law Review*, 109(2), 229–98.

Griffin, D. (2022), *Lexomancy: Law and Magic in the Pseudolegal Writings of the Sovereign Citizen Movement*, Centre for Language and Communication Research, Cardiff University.

Griffin, J., and S. Sardarizadeh, S. (2021), "Nesara: the financial fantasy ruining lives," *BBC World Service*, 21 August 2021: www.bbc.co.uk/programmes/w3ct1xzv.

Gulyas, A. J. (2021), *Conspiracy and Triumph: Theories of a Victorious Future for the Faithful*, McFarland.

Harris, A. P. (2005), "Vultures in eagles' clothing:

conspiracy and racial fantasy in populist legal thought," *Michigan Journal of Race and Law*, 10(2), 269–326.

Hines, A. (2021), "How the Sovereign Citizen Movement convinces desperate parents to ignore laws," *Vice News*, 9 September 2021: www.vice.com/en /article/5db8ak/sovereign-citizens-movement-atta cking-child-protective-services.

Ho, K. (2009), *Liquidated: An Ethnography of Wall Street*, Duke University Press.

Hockett, R. C. (2020), "The capital commons: digital money and citizens' finance in a productive commercial republic," *Review of Banking and Financial Law*, 39, 345–498.

Hodge, E. (2019), "The sovereign ascendant: financial collapse, status anxiety, and the rebirth of the Sovereign Citizen Movement," *Frontiers in Sociology*, 4(76), 1–10.

Howson, P. (2023), *Let Them Eat Crypto: The Blockchain Scam That's Ruining the World*, Pluto Press.

Ingham, G. (2004), *The Nature of Money*, Polity.

Juárez, G. (2021), "The ghostchain. (Or taking things for what they are)," *Paletten*, 325, 54–9.

Juárez, G. (2022), "This is financial advice," *Paletten*, 327–8, 108–11.

Khurana, R. (2007), *From Higher Aims to Hired*

Hands: The Social Transformation of American Business Schools and the Unfulfilled Promise of Management as a Profession, Princeton University Press.

Knight, P. (2000), *Conspiracy Culture: From the Kennedy Assassination to The X-Files*, Routledge.

Komporozos-Athanasiou, A. (2022), *Speculative Communities: Living with Uncertainty in a Financialized World*, University of Chicago Press.

Konda, T. M. (2019), *Conspiracies of Conspiracies: How Delusions Have Overrun America*, University of Chicago Press.

Lamoureux, M. (2022), "Inside the QAnon Queen's cult: 'the abuse was non-stop,'" *Vice News*, 23 August 2022: www.vice.com/en/article/n7ze 5w/qanon-queen-romana-didulo-cult-convoy-ca nada.

Langley, P. (2015), *Liquidity Lost: The Governance of the Global Financial Crisis*, Oxford University Press.

Latour, B. (2017), *Facing Gaia: Eight Lectures on the New Climatic Regime*, Polity.

Lazarus, J. (2020), "Financial literacy education: a questionable answer to the financialization of everyday life," in P. Mader, D. Mertens and N. van der Zwan (eds.), *The Routledge International Handbook of Financialization*, Routledge, 390–9.

Levin, D. L., and M. W. Mitchell (1999), "A law unto themselves: the ideology of the common law court movement," *South Dakota Law Review*, 44(1), 9–40.

Lienau, O. (2014), *Rethinking Sovereign Debt: Politics, Reputation, and Legitimacy in Modern Finance*, Harvard University Press.

Löwy, M. (2009), "Capitalism as religion: Walter Benjamin and Max Weber," *Historical Materialism*, 17(1), 60–73.

Massumi, B. (2018), *99 Theses on the Revaluation of Value: A Postcapitalist Manifesto*, University of Minnesota Press.

Matheson, C. L. (2018), "Psychotic discourse: the rhetoric of the Sovereign Citizen Movement," *Rhetoric Society Quarterly*, 48(2), 187–206.

McKenzie, B., and J. Silverman (2023), *Easy Money: Cryptocurrency, Casino Capitalism, and the Golden Age of Fraud*, Abrams.

McRoberts, C. (2019), "Tinfoil hats and powdered wigs: thoughts on pseudolaw," *Washburn Law Journal*, 58(3), 637–68.

Melley, T. (2000), *Empire of Conspiracy: The Culture of Paranoia in Postwar America*, Cornell University Press.

Mossou, A., and G. Geiger (2022), "As QAnon

falters, European followers flock to a financial conspiracy," *Bellingcat*, 21 December 2022: www.bel
lingcat.com/news/2022/12/21/as-qanon-falters-euro
pean-followers-flock-to-a-financial-conspiracy.

Muniesa, F. (2014), *The Provoked Economy: Economic
Reality and the Performative Turn*, Routledge.

Muniesa, F. (2016), "You must fall down the rabbit
hole," *Journal of Cultural Economy*, 9(3), 316–21.

Muniesa, F. (2017a), "The live act of business and
the culture of realization," *HAU: Journal of Ethnographic Theory*, 7(3), 347–62.

Muniesa, F. (2017b), "On the political vernaculars of
value creation," *Science as Culture*, 26(4), 445–54.

Muniesa, F. (2020), "Business education and anxiety
in the performance of value," in D. Stark (ed.),
*The Performance Complex: Competition and Com-
petitions in Social Life*, Oxford University Press,
260–70.

Muniesa, F. (2022), "Paranoid finance," *Social
Research: An International Quarterly*, 89(3), 731–56.

Muniesa, F. (2023a), "A science of stereotypes:
paranoiac-critical forays within the medium of
information," *Distinktion: Journal of Social Theory*,
24(2), 283–96.

Muniesa, F. (2023b), "Financial value, anthropological critique, and the operations of the law," in

I. Feichtner and G. Gordon (eds.), *Constitutions of Value: Law, Governance, and Political Ecology*, Routledge, 169–80.

Muniesa, F. (2023c), "Revaluation fantasy," *Finance and Society*, 9(1), 73–5.

Netolitzky, D. J. (2018), "Organized pseudolegal commercial arguments as magic and ceremony," *Alberta Law Review*, 55(4), 1045–87.

Netolitzky, D. J. (2019), "After the hammer: six years of Meads v. Meads," *Alberta Law Review*, 56(4), 1167–1207.

Netolitzky, D. J. (2021), "A revolting itch: pseudolaw as a social adjuvant," *Politics, Religion and Ideology*, 22(2), 164–88.

Omarova, S. T. (2021), "The people's ledger: how to democratize money and finance the economy," *Vanderbilt Law Review*, 74(5), 1231–1300.

Ortiz, H. (2014), "The limits of financial imagination: free investors, efficient markets, and crisis," *American Anthropologist*, 116(1), 38–50.

Ortiz, H. (2021), *The Everyday Practice of Valuation and Investment: Political Imaginaries of Shareholder Value*, Columbia University Press.

Pignarre, P., and I. Stengers (2011), *Capitalist Sorcery: Breaking the Spell*, Palgrave Macmillan.

Pistor, K. (2019), *The Code of Capital: How the Law*

Creates Wealth and Inequality, Princeton University Press.

Pitts, F. H. (2021), *Value*, Polity.

Postone, M. (1980), "Anti-Semitism and National Socialism: notes on the German reaction to 'Holocaust,'" *New German Critique*, 19(1), 97–115.

Postone, M. (2017), "The current crisis and the anachronism of value: a Marxian reading," *Continental Thought and Theory: A Journal of Intellectual Freedom*, 1(4), 38–54.

Ricœur, P. (1977), *The Rule of Metaphor: Multidisciplinary Studies of the Creation of Meaning in Language*, University of Toronto Press.

Robé, J.-P. (2020), *Property, Power and Politics: Why We Need to Rethink the World Power System*, Policy Press.

Robertson, D. G. (2016), *UFOs, Conspiracy Theories, and the New Age: Millennial Conspiracism*, Bloomsbury.

Rothschild, M. (2021), *The Storm Is upon Us: How QAnon Became a Movement, Cult, and Conspiracy Theory of Everything*, Melville House.

Rothschild, M. (2023), *Jewish Space Lasers: The Rothschilds and 200 Years of Conspiracy Theories*, Melville House.

Roustang, F. (1987), "How do you make a paranoiac laugh?" *MLN*, 102(4), 707–18.

Samman, A., and S. Sgambati (2023), "Financial eschatology and the libidinal economy of leverage," *Theory, Culture and Society*, 40(3), 103–21.

Sarteschi, C. (2020), *Sovereign Citizens: A Psychological and Criminological Analysis*, Springer.

Sarteschi, C. (2021), "Sovereign citizens: a narrative review with implications of violence towards law enforcement," *Aggression and Violent Behavior*, 60(101509), 1–11.

Shell, M. (1982), *Money, Language, and Thought: Literary and Philosophic Economies from the Medieval to the Modern Era*, University of California Press.

Singh, D. (2018), *Divine Currency: The Theological Power of Money in the West*, Stanford University Press.

Slobodian, Q. (2018), *Globalists: The End of Empire and the Birth of Neoliberalism*, Harvard University Press.

Somers, M. R. (1995), "Narrating and naturalizing civil society and citizenship theory: the place of political culture and the public sphere," *Sociological Theory*, 13(3), 229–74.

Sommer, W. (2023), *Trust the Plan: The Rise of*

QAnon and the Conspiracy that Unhinged America, HarperCollins.

Streeck, W. (2016), *How Will Capitalism End? Essays on a Failing System*, Verso.

Sutter, L. de (2021), *Deleuze's Philosophy of Law*, Edinburgh University Press.

Taillandier, A. (2021), "'Staring into the singularity' and other posthuman tales: transhumanist stories of future change," *History and Theory*, 60(2), 215–33.

Teter, M. (2020), *Blood Libel: On the Trail of an Anti-semitic Myth*, Harvard University Press.

Thomas, Y. (2021), *Legal Artifices: Ten Essays on Roman Law in the Present Tense*, Edinburgh University Press.

Todeschini, G. (2009), "Jews, economic metaphors, and the healthy body politic: the Jewish role in Christian economic narratives and the birth of modern economics," *Jewish History*, 35(3–4), 405–32.

Todeschini, G. (2021), *Franciscan Wealth: From Voluntary Poverty to Market Society*, The Franciscan Institute.

Tooze, A. (2017), "A general logic of crisis," *London Review of Books*, 39(1), 3–8.

Trivellato, F. (2019), *The Promise and Peril of Credit:*

What a Forgotten Legend about Jews and Finance Tells Us about the Making of European Commercial Society, Princeton University Press.

Turner, F. (2006), *From Counterculture to Cyberculture: Stewart Brand, the Whole Earth Network, and the Rise of Digital Utopianism*, University of Chicago Press.

Vogl, J. (2014), *The Specter of Capital*, Stanford University Press.

Vogl, J. (2022), *Capital and Ressentiment: A Short Theory of the Present*, Polity.

Wall, I. R. (2021), *Law and Disorder: Sovereignty, Protest, Atmosphere*, Routledge.

Weir, J. P. (2015), "Sovereign citizens: a reasoned response to the madness," *Lewis and Clark Law Review*, 19(3), 829–68.

Zuboff, S. (2019), *The Age of Surveillance Capitalism: The Fight for a Human Future at the New Frontier of Power*, PublicAffairs.